Bugeaud: a Pack with a Baton

Bugeaud: a Pack with a Baton

The Early Campaigns of a Soldier
of Napoleon's Army Who Would
Become a Marshal of France

Thomas Robert Bugeaud

LEONAUR

Bugeaud: a Pack with a Baton
The Early Campaigns of a Soldier of Napoleon's Army
Who Would Become a Marshal of France
by Thomas Robert Bugeaud

FIRST EDITION

Published by Leonaur Ltd

This book has been adapted by the Leonaur editors from
Memoirs of Marshal Bugeaud Vol. 1
edited by the Count H. d'Ideville
English edition edited from the French by Charlotte M. Yonge
Published by Hurst & Blackett, 1884

ISBN: 978-1-84677-247-4 (hardcover)
ISBN: 978-1-84677-248-1 (softcover)

http://www.leonaur.com

Publisher's Note

The opinions expressed in this book are those of the author
and are not necessarily those of the publisher.

Contents

Publisher's Note

Thomas Robert Bugeaud, the youngest of thirteen children, was born in 1784 at Limoges, France, into a noble family of Périgord. As a very young man he ran away from home, and lived for some years as an agricultural worker. At the age of twenty, impoverished and without rank or status, he began to think about his future—he loved agriculture, but decided that it held little prospect for establishing himself in the world; he considered the church, but that held no attraction for him at all; then he reluctantly decided that a military career offered the best chance of making his name.

In 1804 Bugeaud became a private soldier in the *vélites* of the Imperial Guard, but it was not a career he relished, and for much of his military life he yearned to return to the land and the bucolic pursuits he loved. In the following year he took part in the Austerlitz campaign and early in 1806, he received a commission as a sub-lieutenant. He served in the Jena and Eylau campaigns, won promotion to the rank of lieutenant at the battle of Pultusk in December 1806. Bugeaud was a member of the first French corps to enter Spain in 1808, and was stationed in Madrid during the revolt of the Dos Mayo. At the Second Siege of Saragossa, he again won promotion—to the rank of captain.

In 1809/1810 Bugeaud distinguished himself under the generalship of Marshal Suchet in the eastern theatre of the Peninsular War, and was soon promoted to the rank of major and the command of a full regiment At the first restoration of the Bourbons he was made a colonel, but he rejoined Napoleon during the Hundred Days, and again, under the command of his old patron Suchet, he distinguished himself in the war in the Alps.

By 1815 Bugeaud, still a young man, found he had no place in the army; he returned to Périgord and again took to agriculture. It was during this period that he became a noted agricultural reformer and agronomist.

In 1830 Bugeaud was once more called upon to serve his country in a military capacity, a period during which he again served with distinction. He later entered politics, became governor-general of Algeria, was made a Marshal of France and was created Duke d'Isly after his great victory at Isly in 1844.

As a great military leader, over almost fifty years, Bugeaud left his mark on France, Europe and North Africa, but it is his early career that made the man. This Leonaur book, largely based on letters to his family, concerns itself with Bugeaud's military service in those early years as a soldier in the Napoleonic wars—a period of just eleven years, during which he fought for Napoleon in Austria, Poland, the Peninsula and the Alps, and showed himself to be a brilliant, if reluctant, soldier, and a natural leader of men.

The Leonaur Editors

In the following text comments by the book's
original editor are inset in smaller type

CHAPTER 1

Birth and Childhood

Born at Limoges, October 15, 1784, Thomas Robert Bugeaud de la Piconnerie was the son of a gentleman of Périgord, Jean-Ambroise Bugeaud, noble, Marquis de la Piconnerie, and of Françoise de Sutton de Clonard, a member of an Irish family which settled in France with James II. According to a letter addressed to the Editor of the *Tribune*, in 1844, the Marshal ironically traced his genealogy to a rather plebeian source. 'My grandfather,' he there says, 'was a smith; with his sturdy arms, and by scorching his own eyes and hands, he gained a fortune, that my father, an idle aristocrat, employed in a spirited manner.' Two genuine documents, the register of the Marshal's birth, and his father's marriage contract, establish his paternity with precision.

Of the marriage of Jean-Ambroise Bugeaud de la Piconnerie with Mdlle. de Clonard were born fourteen children, of whom seven lived: Patrice de la Piconnerie, Ambroise de la Piconnerie, Thomassine de la Piconnerie, married the Vicomte d'Orthez, Phillis de la Piconnerie, married M. de Puyssegenez, de Lignac, Helene de la Piconnerie, married M. Sermensan, Antoinette de la Piconnerie, married M. de St. Germain and Thomas-Robert Bugeaud de la Piconnerie.

Patrice Bugeaud, the eldest brother of the Marshal, had married Mdlle. Durand d'Auberoche, daughter of the Vicomte d'Auberoche, of a very ancient family of Périgord. Ambroise de la Piconnerie, an officer like his elder brother Patrice, served in the army of the Princes during the emigration. He lost his life by shipwreck on the way to India with his regiment. The Vicomte d'Orthez, husband of Thomassine, was descended in direct line from the Count d'Orthez, Governor of Bayonne, who refused to have the Protestants murdered on the occasion of the Saint Bartholomew. A Sutton de Clonard, brother of Madame de la Piconnerie, the Marshal's mother, was lost with La Peyrouse, being second in command.

Lastly, Thomas Bugeaud, Marshal of France, married in 1818 Mdlle. de Lafaye. The Marshal left two daughters and a son; the elder married to M. Gasson; the younger married General Count Feray, who died in 1870. The Marshal's only son, Charles, Duke d'Isly, married Mdlle. O de Saint Paul, and died childless in 1868. All the grandchildren of Marshal Bugeaud are authorised to bear his name.

Although several members of his family had emigrated in the years following 1789, the Marquis de la Piconnerie, after his release from the prison at Limoges, did not think of leaving France. The Marshal's childhood was far from being happy. His father, an old gentleman, harsh and selfish, ruined by the Revolution, had banished his daughters and little son to La Durantie, while he continued to reside at Limoges with his eldest son Patrice, upon whom he concentrated all his affection. The notes of the Comtesse Feray upon her father's childhood must be given without alteration:

My father was born at Limoges, in a hotel of the Eue de la Cruche d'Or, in old Limoges, once the aristocratic quarter. A marble tablet marks the house, which is now turned into a shop.

He was the fourteenth child of the Marquis de la Piconnerie. Being intended for the Church, he entered into the world with the title of Monsieur l'Abbé. At six years old he was removed from his nurse's care, a fine child; his father ordered a handsome dress for him, and sent him to school, where he made rapid progress.

One year later, in 1791, all the circumstances of the family were changed; the Revolution had broken out; my grandfather, grandmother, and their youngest daughter, Antoinette, were in prison; their elder sons had emigrated. Thomassine, my eldest aunt, was married to the Count d'Orthez; and the younger children were left alone, and were obliged to work in order to support their imprisoned parents. Phillis, then aged sixteen, and her sister Hélène, without a moment's hesitation, began to make shirts from morning till night. Their brother, who was not yet eight years old, cooked, ran errands, and took home the work when it was finished.

My aunt Phillis was frequently summoned to appear before the revolutionary tribunal, as her beauty had made an impression upon the monsters. Therefore she always took her little brother with her as a companion; and both of them showed so much quiet courage, that they managed to gain the respect of these men, and thus, thanks to them, the condemnation of their parents was delayed. However, notwithstanding their efforts, the sentence had been pronounced, and the day fixed for the execution of M. and Mdme. de la Piconnerie, when the news of Robespierre's death saved them from the scaffold.

When my grandmother was released from prison, she made her youngest son resume his studies. We have been told that a few days before the school prize-giving she had a vision at night. Her father and mother, the Count and Countess de Clonard, drew the curtains of her bed, took her by the hand, and said, 'Daughter, prepare to come and join us in heaven; you will die in four days' time.' The very hour was fixed. My grandmother, without any weakness, performed all her Christian duties, and, after having been a spectator of her little Thomas's success, went home, and died on the day and at the hour named by the phantoms.

My grandfather, whose fortune was but small, had been nearly ruined by the Revolution. He sent his daughters to the Château of La Durantie, and stayed at Limoges with his eldest son Patrice, the only one about, whom he ever concerned himself. As for the youngest born, he never greatly cared for him. In times gone by, such was often the fate of younger sons.

My grandfather was a man with a terrible temper, and is still the theme of legend in that part of the country. Our country-folk are convinced that long after his death ho walked the woods of Durantie by night, followed by a fierce pack of hounds and a troop of gentlemen. These honest folk declare that they can hear his voice roaring like thunder beneath the branches of the forest, and say that his great white horse, with fiery red eyes, can be seen from far by the light of the moon. It is to be hoped that our grandfather now rests in peace.

Patrice, like his father, was proud and violent; otherwise both of them had their amiable moments. Phillis, the eldest (unmarried) sister, was as beautiful as a statue, with an expression full of high spirit, yet of calmness. She would have been remarkable in the loftiest station, but her views were bounded by doing good, or by glorying in her brother Thomas, whom she had brought-up, and whom she almost worshipped.

Hélène, with lovely features and golden locks, had a feminine style of beauty; her ready and gracious intelligence adapted itself to all the circumstances and needs of life. The saying of her in the family was, 'Fit for the king's court or the poultry-court.'

Antoinette was small and plain, but very good. Her sparkling wit, her vivacity, and astonishing memory, were the delight of the family, and her death left a great gap among us.

Ambroise, a naval officer, whom his sisters often compared to my father, died at twenty-five in the expedition of La Peyrouse.

The Château de la Durantie, near de la Nouaille, Dordogne, was in old times inhabited by my grandfather's brothers, priests or old bachelors, and his sisters, old spinsters, and nuns driven from the Convents of Périgueux and Limoges during the tempest of the Revolution.

My grandfather had twenty-three brothers and sisters. His mother, childless for five years, went on pilgrimage to the celebrated Virgin of Rocamadour in Lot. It is to be observed that her prayer was more than granted.

My father was attended to by no one at Limoges, for the Marquis and Patrice hardly ever spoke to him at all. He had been taken away from school after his mother's death, and was learning scarcely anything. He was lonely and felt forsaken by everyone, but he endured his privations with resignation.

But one day, in despair at the state of isolation in which he was kept, he left a note for his father to say that he had gone to his sisters, obtained a bit of bread from the servants, and when evening, came quitted Limoges. He walked all night, went the whole way on foot (eight-and-forty miles), reached La Durantie worn out, but overjoyed to see his sisters: he was then thirteen years old.

This poor habitation bore the name of the Château de la Durantie, no doubt traditionally, in remembrance of the old homes of the family. In remote ages there had been a feudal castle at La Piconnerie, a few hundred yards away from La Durantie, supposed to have been destroyed during the English invasion, but I am not sure enough of the fact to assert it. The only thing that I am certain of is, that it did exist; even in 1840 I saw a tower in the middle of the farm. The plan of this manor is among the documents in the possession of our cousin, the Marquis de la Piconnerie. The family had lived in the Château de la Gandumas and at La Durantie for infinite ages. After my grandfather it was only called Old Durantie. It was a long, narrow house, with an outbuilding attached to it, equally long and narrow, consisting of a ground-floor and loft. A building opposite completed a large square court, enclosed towards the road by a wooden paling.

The house was entered by a low door studded with great nails, leading into a vestibule paved with little pebbles. Opposite was the granary door, with a little hole for the cats in the bottom. Inside this door an almost perpendicular stair led to the wheat-store. On the right of the vestibule, another door opened into a great kitchen also pitched with pebbles; in the middle was a very large table with benches round it; on the wall to the right was a beautifully carved wooden cupboard, reaching to the ceiling, which had once contained the pewter vessels with the family arms. There was a soup stove in a corner; then some immense provision chests, black with age. The whole of one side of the old kitchen was taken up by a wide and deep fire-place. This was the foresters' favourite place, where they dried themselves of an evening by the flames of enormous faggots, with their dogs between their knees. A window looking on the court gave a view of anything that was going on. To the right of the vestibule was the parlour, or rather the common hall. This had what I cannot call a floor, but a sort of badly jointed planking. A sideboard took up the whole of one wall; and a glazed door opening to the garden made this room tolerably cheerful in summer. A window in front looked out on the court; at the back was a high chimney-piece with some pretence at panelling. As ornaments upon it in summer, great bunches of daffodils and honeysuckle were displayed in the old earthenware vases; in winter a row of enormous beetroots, some fine apples, and little sheaves of ears of curious sorts of corn. In the middle of the room stood a long thick table of wax-polished walnut, some chairs, and two arm-chairs of straw. These two arm-chairs represented all the comfort of the habitation.

To the right of the fireplace was the room of the head of the family; to the left a small door opening on a long and narrow corridor that led to three large rooms in the back building. The lower one was reached by a passage open to all the winds of heaven. It was the most elegant, there was a looking-glass above the chimney-piece; and the two grand old beds, hung with magnificent silk drapery, probably a remnant of the furniture from Limoges, were not in harmony with the rustic simplicity of the dwelling.

On the other side of the quadrangle a large building contained the cellar, the workshops of all sorts, and the corn-stores. The well, surrounded by a stone trough for watering the cattle, was opposite the house door. Lastly, the court was full of fowls, ducks, and turkeys, not forgetting the great manure-heap. And this was the dwelling where my father's youth was passed in company with his sisters.

Of his uncles, several had gone to America to seek their fortune, others had remained under the headship of the second brother, M. de la Durantie. Two or three sisters were married. Mdlles. de Saint Martin and des Places had remained in the nest, with nothing but their spinning-wheels to amuse them. At Durantie my father lived like Robinson Crusoe; rising at dawn to go out to the chase, he came back at dinner-time in triumph, almost always bringing back some game, as an addition to the family fare, which, as usual, was chiefly composed of chestnuts. When resting he worked with his sisters, who taught him, poor girls, all that they recollected of their learning in the convent. They learnt Molière and Racine by heart together, and then acted the scenes, giving each other the cue. Forty years afterwards, my father and one of my aunts gave us a recitation of a dialogue of Molière, which they had repeated in their youth, and did not miss a single word. After lessons the little brother went off to fish, enlisting the little country boys of his own age in his wanderings. They all remained faithful to him, and most of them died as farmers upon the property. He did not trouble himself much about meals; a fire of dead branches was soon lighted to cook chestnuts or potatoes from the fields, or he would seek the hospitality of the farmhouses, where the little master was universally known and beloved. My father has told me that he had no leather shoes; wooden ones were very soon worn out in this active life, so he invented a way of making sandals out of cherry bark and string, which were a complete success. His sisters had no shoes, and spent months without going out.

My father was in great trouble at an invitation to a wedding at a house in the neighbourhood, where there were to be all the amusements of that good old time. It was impossible to attend in his dress of patched grey cloth. Just as, with swelling heart, he was about to send a refusal, he remembered he had seen, in an old chest in the loft, the dress that an ancestor had worn at the Court of Louis XV. With his sisters' help, he brushed the dust off the suit, and the dear girls soon contrived to attire their little brother. He had never seen himself so fine in his life, and off he went to the much-desired feast, where he danced three days with a success that made him very proud.

At La Durantie the quiet life of the girls and their little brother was only occasionally interrupted by the rare visits of my grandfather and uncle Patrice. Everything trembled before the lord and master. His children were never allowed to speak to him unless he interrogated them. One day my grandfather was giving an order to a servant about some farming matter. My father, then fifteen, thoughtlessly allowed himself to make a remark. The marquis in a fury lifted a great stick he had in his hand against the boy. My father, in a fright at his audacity, and foreseeing the results of the paternal anger, jumped out of his great wooden shoes and ran away to avoid the blow. My grandfather stumbled over his son's heavy foot-gear and the club gave the wall a violent blow.

My father had tears in his eyes when he told us of our grandfather's harshness. 'Never,' has he said, 'did he once give me a single caress, and I never remember his giving me a single kiss. I do delight to caress you, my dear children, and therefore I lavish upon you the tenderness that was so much missed by my loving heart.' Poor father!

After his mother's death the boy met with no affection save from his sisters, who loved him like mothers. However, he easily consoled himself, thanks to his passion for the chase and for life in the open air. One winter night, in beautiful moonlight, he was on the watch for a fox not far from the house, and seeing in the wood a whole flight of woodcocks waddling over the hardened snow he thought the sight so charming that he ran to the house, and, notwithstanding the cold, made his sisters get out of bed to partake of these sportsman's pleasures.

CHAPTER 2

Private Soldier (1804)

However, time went on. Thomas Bugeaud was nearly eighteen years old. Country life, sport, and study, were no longer enough for him. He felt the necessity of making a future. Considering that he had no patron to advance him in the world, and being unwilling to leave his own country, he applied for a clerk's desk to M. Festugières, who had married the elder sister of Mdlle. Elisabeth de Lafaye, who afterwards became his wife. M. Festugières was owner of some considerable ironworks in Périgord. He had a long interview with the young man, and told him: 'My boy, I do not want a gentleman as clerk, it is not a situation for you; your ability should raise you into high rank in the army. Go into it since you are not well off.' Thomas, in despair, went home to embrace his sisters, started for Limoges, and in a couple of days his lot as a soldier was fixed.

The following letter was written by Thomas Bugeaud a short time before his enlistment. His hesitation shows how little taste he had for a wandering life of adventure:

<u>To his sister Phillis Bugeaud de la Piconnerie</u>

La Durantie, May, 1804: I did not answer your last letter immediately, because I was waiting for Patrice to ask his advice, and come to a decision one way or other. After we had both reached the conclusion that the best course to adopt for the present is what you have been kind enough to suggest, I ceased to hesitate.

I considered that, perhaps, in fourteen or fifteen months' time I might be obliged to go, and then so much time would be lost. If in three or four years I have no taste for a military career, I could take my discharge, and then be able to enter another profession. So, my dear Phillis, I have made my decision, and expect to go away about Easter. Will you be kind enough to send me the letter of introduction you promised, and also tell me all you think about my intention?

Though you say so, my dear, I do not think I can *walk alone*. I am not so conceited yet. You cannot know much of me if you think that I did not want your advice. No, my dear, I never meant to say so. I want it—a great deal of it. I only said that you could not make me see blue black, and black blue. Anyhow, you have always the same right over my heart and mind.

I am very sorry that I have not the means to come and see you before I go away. But you know, my dear, that I have hardly any money. I have already spent nearly all my year's allowance on the necessary outfit and in my illness. I am not quite well yet, and have returns of fever. I hope to be quite cured by the first fine weather, and to be able to start.

How I wish Bordeaux was on my road, or not far from it. How delighted I should be to go and wish you goodbye; but, alas! you are in the south and I am in the north.

However, I hope not to be parted from you for ever, and reckon upon presenting you in a few years with a brother worthy of you.

No doubt you think my writing very bad. Since I had the fever, I have quite lost the habit of writing, and must form my hand again.

Adieu, my love. Answer me at once. Kiss Helen and Edward, and give them a million compliments for me. Do not omit to give my remembrances to my aunt and cousins.

It is to his elder sister Phillis, his faithful and devoted confidante, that the youngest son of the Marquis de la Piconnerie almost always addresses himself. There is nothing concealed from her; he tells her all his impressions, his most secret thoughts, all that he does; and we know nothing more touching than this tender and filial attachment of the young brother to her who stood to him in the place of a mother, and in whose company were spent his early years in the old home of La Durantie.

The sincere affection expressed by the young Bugeaud towards his sister Phillis never diminished. The Comtesse de Puyssegenetz all her life retained the ascendancy she had possessed over her brother during his infancy and youth. We have heard an affecting anecdote on this subject.

A short time before his death, Marshal Bugeaud at a family dinner at La Durantie had a little discussion with his elder sister. Without intending it he had certainly vexed his dear sister a little, so that a little pearl of a tear appeared in her eye. Seeing this, the Marshal jumped up, and throwing himself on his sister's neck, himself burst into tears. 'Oh, my dear Phillis, oh, my well-beloved, can it really be I that have made you weep? I shall never forgive myself.'

Thomas Bugeaud enlisted at Fontainebleau on the 29th of June, 1804, in the foot grenadiers of the Imperial Guard (corps of the *vélites*), being nineteen years and some months of age. Appointment to the *vélites* of the guard was a little favour to the young Limousin recruit. The corps of *vélites* was composed of young soldiers of a little more education than the rest, and the First Consul intended that it should be a nursery for sub-officers.

The Comtesse Feray observes:

Barrack-life was a time of suffering to my father. The future did not look bright to him, having neither friends nor money. He spent in study all the time he had left from fatigues and drill. He even sold some of his bread to buy books. He had not money enough to buy candles. When his comrades were asleep, he read by the smoky barrack lights. He was very often hungry, and in his dreams feasted upon the chestnuts and mealy potatoes of old Durantie. As a recruit, he was very badly treated by the veterans; his fine white hands, some marks of the small-pox, his beardless chin, red hair, and especially his taste for books, were the subjects for continual attack, while discipline compelled him to be silent.

At that time the soldiers had only one soup-bowl between six men. It was set upon a form or table; the men made a ring round it, and there was a rule by which they ate. Each in turn put in his wooden spoon, and abstained while the others took their share. One day my father, in his hunger, forgot the regulation, and when he had swallowed one spoonful took another at once. On this one of the "old grumblers" rushed at the glutton, and shouted at him in a rage, "With your *thématiques* and *gérographie* you are only a confounded greenhorn."

Upon this he received the contents of the bowl in his face. A duel* ensued; the old grenadier was killed; and from that day the young recruits, hitherto martyrs and butts, were treated with much more respect in the regiment.

Although he was experiencing a time of peace, my father

---

* This was his first duel. We are told that his second was during the campaign in Austria, when a rough sergeant commanding the detachment talked of offering insult to the daughters of a house where they had been hospitably entertained, Corporal Bugeaud exclaimed against such dastardly conduct; a duel was the instant result, and the sergeant killed on the spot. A third, we have to mention, took place long after, in 1832, when the Deputy Dulong was killed.

felt little inclination for the profession of arms. He kept on writing to his sisters, lamenting the poverty that had driven him from his home. His greatest consolation was to go and sit at the foot of a tree in the forest of Fontainebleau, and pour forth his tears. He has told us:"I was one day in a miserable state, when a comrade saw me. 'What are you about, you fool? Do not cry like a calf; come to the laundresses' ball.' He dragged me along, and I was still wretched when we went in. My comrade knew the ways of the place, he gave a nod to the prettiest girls; and then I was in the middle of them, and my melancholy soon put to flight in the whirl of a waltz. I was mad for dancing. The ball did me a great deal of good, and I did not go so often to pour out my sorrows to the wilds of the forest.'"

The two following letters, written from Fontainebleau and Courbevoie by the young *vélite* of the guard to his sister Phillis, show that he was already meeting the miseries of his condition more patiently:

To his sister Phillis

Fontainebleau, 11 Thermidor, 1804: I was anxiously expecting your letter, and at last it has come. But for that I should not even now be reconciled to my profession; but now that you approve, I am content, and am vexed at nothing but the separation from you. I begin to have a better idea of the views of the government about our corps. Generals are often sent to see if we are doing well, and inspect our progress. Marshal Bessiéres reviewed us yesterday; he promised us masters, and it is almost certain that in a fortnight everything will be arranged. I am delighted at this. I have got back a great deal of my taste for study, and am really afraid, because drill and duty leave me so little time for learning. But in three or four months we shall know our drill, and then have much more time. A man could make very little progress with only the corps masters. There will be so many of us, that each one could hardly have a ten minutes' lesson, so that I intend to have a private master for each subject that I take up in public. That is the way to get distinction. I have but little hope of advance till M. Blondeau gets a place. The first-come *vélites* have all the best of it; they have attracted the observation of the chiefs before us, and already some forty of them have been appointed instructors, and they will soon become sub-officers.

It is hard enough to become acquainted with the chiefs. They are afraid of making us jealous of one another by seeming to patronise any of us. Another thing is that there are only two of our officers whose society is in any way desirable; the others are good soldiers, but men of low birth and small means. However, I intend to do my best to do duty well with them, for a man must make himself known; without that he would always hang in a rut. I expect to make acquaintance with a young captain by means of the chase, for he is very fond of it.,1 have already got myself mentioned to him by a sergeant whom I know. I have spoken of myself as a great sportsman, and I hope that I shall soon go out with him. When we have been after game two or three times together, we shall be good friends.

It is still more difficult to make respectable acquaintance in the town. The *soldier* is in very bad repute. There is great distrust of anyone who wears uniform; and not remembering that the frock does not make the friar, people will hardly meet any of us in society, not even the superior officers. I have been told that there was only one *vélite* who mixed in good society at Fontainebleau, and that was because he had relations there. The chief cause of our banishment from honourable society is, that several *vélites* have insulted women, and otherwise misconducted themselves in many ways. And so we are reduced to the society of low women and barmaids. I hope you do not suppose I frequent it. When I have a spare moment I prefer to pass it in barracks, or in the room I have hired, in reading and learning English and geography. I have bought a dictionary from Paris. Even if I were disposed to dissipation, I have no time for it. We are obliged to be so very clean—both our arms and our persons—that we have to work without ceasing. We have at the outside an hour a-day, so you need not be afraid of the mother of all the vices. I never was more well-disposed, and in a corps of grenadiers I am behaving, perhaps, much better than I should in a hermitage. I go to mass on Sunday morning, and hear a sermon on that day, as much for pleasure as for piety. I sometimes say prayers, and have never been laughed at by my comrades for it. Several more do the same as I do, and the others do not deride them.

There are a great many of these young men who are not of good family, sons of peasants and artisans; there are also some of high birth, but in general this corps is not what is supposed. There is very little intimacy among the *vélites*; we meet and look at one another like strangers, and do not make up large parties. Each has two or three friends, with whom he goes out and shares his pleasures. We are not incited to expense, or asked to do evil.

The discipline is very strict and very harsh. There is an order against playing billiards; if a young man is known to have lost even so little money he is very sharply reprimanded. We have to be in by nine o'clock, and if late, are confined to barracks; if the offence is repeated, the guard-room.

Our chiefs all have very bad principles; they believe that after death there is an end of everything, that they are beasts like the rest; they believe in a Supreme Being, but suppose He is neutral. This is the language of all I have spoken to, and they introduced the subject. Unfortunately, there are only too many young men disposed to listen to them.

I hope, my dear, that I shall follow your wise counsels without difficulty, and that when Heaven grants me the favour of seeing you again, you will find me virtuous, and thankful for the great share you will have had in my good conduct, and the advice you have given me, and I hope will give me.

I have found X—— so little inclined to give me what he himself acknowledges my parents left me, that I have not ventured to ask him for any more. We have come to no arrangement. I sold him my linen, and the price, together with what he owed me, amounts to five hundred francs. I asked him to advance me the first six months of my allowance, and he refused, saying I was foolish; but he promised not to let me be in want, and to send me my allowance punctually. You may imagine that after paying for my journey, staying thirteen days in Paris at an hotel with M. Blondeau, buying several things I wanted, such as books, paper, *nankeen* breeches, dimity waistcoats, silver buckles, hat, uniform, and a lot of things necessary not to look like a beggar, I can have very little left; and I am afraid that X—— will not be in a hurry to send me any more. With the strictest economy, and spending nothing but what is necessary—like paying my masters—I shall find it difficult to wait two months. X—— thought that five hundred francs would be enough for my expenses, as having nothing to buy; he is very much mistaken. Besides that we have to pay something to the masters over us, there is a good deal to spend on our kit. We are allowed to make our uniform as handsome as we like. After duty is over, one can only go out in *nankeen* breeches, silk or fine cotton stockings, or with *kerseymere* pantaloons, and boots. It is only the rustics who go out differently dressed; and the way to gain notice is to show that one is not a man without means, and to be well appointed, M. Blondeau, who understands the case, strongly advised me to attend to this. I give you these particulars, so that you may not think I spend my money badly.

A thousand things to all, and my respects to my aunt. Adieu, my love; I am everything that a good brother should be to Hélène.

To his sister Phillis

Fontainebleau, 10 Fructidor, 1804: The recommendation you mention might be of great service to me, though it is not often that this kind of patronage is successful, because all the men in power receive so many requests that they scarcely pay attention to them. However, those that come from a brother ought to be a little better received; so I beg of you not to neglect it. I should prefer the letter being addressed to General Bessières himself, as it is very difficult to present such a thing to a man of his rank. He knows me already, for he received me at Fontainebleau, the last time he went there with the Emperor.

If he is reminded of this, and would like to be of service to me, he can easily find me. I should be very glad to be in the theoretical class; those who have been taken into it are almost sure to be made sub-officers, as they are learning the duties. No one has been chosen who had no interest; ability and talents count for nothing. More than three-quarters of them are worth very little, while in our corps there are many educated young men to be found who are not the least thought of.

I have not lost hopes of getting into good society. I have made the acquaintance of the lady from whom I have hired a room. She is the wife of a printer; but in this part of the country women of that class have a much better tone than they have among us even in far higher rank. She has promised to introduce me to the sets that will be made up at the beginning of winter; she will get me invitations to balls and concerts; and when I am there, I shall try gradually to form friendships, and, perhaps, shall manage to get myself a good 'bourgeois' society.

Our commanding officer gave us a very agreeable surprise the other day. After drilling us about a great deal, he said he was so pleased with us that he would take us out for a march. And so we marched off, but had hardly gone a quarter of a mile, when we saw some baskets full of bread, bottles, cheese, and sausages. We jumped for joy at this sight, and when the commandant had made us pile arms, we formed groups, and made a capital breakfast. We toasted the commandant, our chiefs, and the glory of France. I went to him, and in the name of my comrades paid him a little compliment on the feast that he was giving us. he seemed pleased, and put into my hands a great Brie cheese and a hamper of Burgundy to share among us. When we had done eating we had a dance to beat of drum.

This, my dear Phillis, is the only pleasant moment I have had since I have been here. This little scene has given me a little taste for the army, and I felt almost for the first time a slight breath of ambition.

Adieu, my dear Phillis; do not make me languish any more. If you knew all the pleasure you give me you would make great haste to send an answer. I hope you do not want fresh assurances to believe that I feel like the most affectionate of brothers to you.

The serious and candid side of this character is well displayed in these private confidences and by his bitter regrets at the difficulty of obtaining education. This desire to learn appears in all his letters. Indeed it was to himself

27

the Marshal owed all he knew. During the troubled period of the Revolution and under the Directory it was almost impossible for a boy—for a young man without means, and living in the country, to obtain any thorough education. We have seen above that such an abode as La Durantie was little fitted to enlarge the circle of ideas and knowledge of the son of the Marquis de la Piconnerie. And so our homage is due to the perseverance and force of will of the young man from Périgord, ardently desirous to study, blushing for his ignorance, and attaining through his own exertions alone a very fair amount of information for a soldier of fortune. Afterwards he did a great deal to supply the want of early education; and if he had not the 'culture that results from close study,' as General Trochu rather severely regrets, he made up for these imperfections by some very superior qualities.

CHAPTER 3

The Coronation (1804)

In the letters which follow the young brother continues to make a confidante of his beloved Phillis. His whole character is revealed in these private outpourings; the little *vélite* is still somewhat shy and haughty, and his taste for 'the military,' as he calls it, diminishes every day instead of increasing. His weariness and distaste for the regiment is more evident, and is so strong that the enlisted volunteer thinks of entering the Military School. But the cost is considerable, the eldest brother, Patrice, rather hard, and Thomas, alas! could not meet such heavy expenses with the very small fortune left him by the Marquis de la Piconnerie.

TO HIS SISTER PHILLIS

Since my last letter I have had several little adventures, both good and bad. I remember you told me to try to approach my chiefs. Well, my dear, I have done it, whether I would or no, and that in a way that might have kept me still more aloof. I do not know if I have told you that I had a friend of the name of Lamothe. This friend had a dispute, and asked me to be his second. I could not refuse, though there is a special order against fighting or being a second. As we were on our way to the appointed place we were arrested by the guard. Lamothe and his adversary were put in the guard-room, and I was left at large till further orders.

As soon as the two combatants were together they had a desperate battle, and would no doubt have throttled each other had they not been parted. The commandant was very angry, and intended to punish them very severely; but as some one pointed out to him that Lamothe was not to blame, as he had been insulted, he suspended the punishment, and desired Lamothe and me to give our facts and reasons in writing. My friend was unable to write because he had sprained his wrist in the struggle, and so he asked me to do it for him; and so I made myself up into a Demosthenes to plead his defence and mine.

You know that among the blind the one-eyed is king. The chiefs who are good soldiers, who have obtained their position by bravery and nothing else, considered that what I said was splendid, and acquitted both of us. Since that time their manner to me is changed, and the commandant often speaks to me. Of late he addressed me in a very friendly way, asked me several questions as to my position, the way I was treated by the inferior chiefs, and a number of other things. I told him that I was very well satisfied, because it is a bad plan to complain. Then he said to me, 'You are one of my recruits, Monsieur de la Piconnerie. I presented you to General Bessiéres.'

I did not fail to give him the credit, nor to manifest my gratitude. Then he tapped me on the shoulder, and repeatedly promised that he would not forget me. He also asked, 'You can write well, Monsieur de la Piconnerie?'

'Very little, commandant, but if my small talents could be of any use to you, I should be most happy to place them at your disposal'

He accepted this, and has employed me several times, and so I have had the pleasure of seeing his daughters, who are very ladylike.

You see, my dear Phillis, that I have reason to hope that

I shall not be forgotten when there are places going among the *vélites*, for the commandant is all-powerful, and will be referred to in the selection of persons. I am very glad of this, though not ambitious.

My love for soldiering, instead of increasing, diminishes every day, and I am come to hoping that I may not always remain a private soldier if only for the sake of being less unhappy. Perhaps at a future time I shall think differently; but it is such a hard case, one is such a slave, and under so many persons who generally abuse one, that a man has to be absolutely without feeling—like a bit of marble—if he is to be a soldier. I can tell you, my dear, that 'the military' is a fine school for patience, and just the thing to form the character. I have a notion that when you see me again I shall be as gentle as a lamb.

Patrice is mistaken in saying that I am making progress in mathematics; I only told him that I was studying them. How could I get on when I have so little time to myself? Our labours are not lessened, and, I fancy, will not diminish till after the coronation of the Emperor, for as we are to go to Paris for it, the commandant has set his heart on making us drill as well as the oldest grenadiers.

As for English, I work very little at it. At last a master for drawing, grammar, and writing, has been given to us; but it is difficult to get on in these general schools, for the numbers are too great. We are more than three hundred in the drawing-class: so I have determined to engage the same master for my private lessons.

To his sister Phillis

Fontainebleau, 1804: For the last few days we have been journeying to Paris, and I am very much tired, for we carried our packs, and I had loaded myself very much, expecting to remain several days. But we were not even given time to rest.

31

We arrived in the evening, next day were reviewed by the Emperor, and manoeuvred a long time before His Majesty, who was said to be much pleased with us. Next day we went off again. I had hardly time to speak to M. Blondeau. He was very friendly, and by his advice and conversation gave me a little of the encouragement I stood in great need of. He promised to write to me as soon as he has succeeded, so that I may go to see him at Paris, where he expects to be very useful to me. I forgot in my last letter to give you the account you asked me for, and will do so now.

It is true that I am thinking of the Military School, because when once a man is there he is sure of getting out with the rank of sub-lieutenant, and can really learn there, for the authorities do not, as with us, attend only to making the lads go to drill, but also to giving them the knowledge necessary for making good officers—real soldiers, for an ignorant officer is unworthy of the name. It is true that in that school a most severe slavery has to be endured for a year or eighteen months, but I should be glad to part with my liberty for that time if I determine to follow the military profession. I stand well with my chiefs, and am as happy as possible, for a soldier. I am most kindly treated. But what vexes me is that they reckon too much upon my complaisance, and that there is not a moment when I am not overloaded with work; so that with all the racket of barracks I can scarcely secure a moment for my mathematical master. To make up for this I have been excused from guard-mounting and patrol duty, and am very glad of it. I have been appointed an instructor; and have to study the soldiers' schooling, and be present at a two-hours' lesson. As I have begun so long after the others, I must work hard to catch them up. I fully expect that for three months I shall not be able to study some most essential things.

The names of my principal chiefs are Commandant Chéry, Adjutant-Major Véjut, he is from Lyons, and the Commandant from near Fontainebleau. The General commanding the corps is named Ulat. Marshal Bessières is the General-in-Chief—at least I think so, for he has often reviewed us.

The following letter mentions some memorable scenes at which Bugeaud was present:

To his sister Phillis

Fontainebleau, 25 Primaire, 1804: I was expecting your letter with impatience, but not grumbling: I will never come to that; I am too sure of you to fear anything. So it is no use to talk any more sentiment—we are not obliged to pour it out in every letter; let us keep to history, and leave our hearts to take care of the rest, giving them *carte blanche*.

I have seen a quantity of things that were new to me. The Emperor came, as you know, to Fontainebleau to receive the Pope. I had the pleasure of seeing him several times very close when he went hunting. He even spoke to me, and asked me if there were many *vélites* in a detached barrack he was passing. I answered him, saluting. He acknowledged my salute, and passed on with the speed of lightning. A few days afterwards he met the Pope, and brought him back in his carriage. Every evening I went and walked in the castle-yard to look at the Court equipages, and though I have long been excused from guard-mounting, I asked to go on, in hopes of being posted in the Emperor's or Empress's ante-room. It was as I expected. I found myself on sentry at the apartments of Madame Bonaparte. I saw her several times, and had a quarter of an hour's talk with a lady of her suite, very pretty and amiable.

The same day the Emperor went hunting. A stag was taken, and the *curée* performed in the castle-yard in His Majesty's presence. More than two hundred hounds threw themselves upon the poor creature, and he was eaten up in a moment. You may imagine whether I admired the sight!

We gave a grand banquet to our brothers-in-arms who had come with the Emperor. Everything went off gaily, and more than one bottle of wine was emptied in drinking our health. We went to Paris to be present at His Majesty's coronation; it lasted ten or twelve days. We had a great deal of trouble, and no pleasure at all. The weather was very bad, we were heavily loaded, and, to complete our misfortunes, we had to go beyond Paris, and occupy barracks four miles from the city. At every festival we remained the whole day under arms; it was very cold, and the mud abominable. At the end of the day we returned to our infernal barrack, and had to work like negroes to clean our arms and tidy ourselves for the next day. This, my dear, is the pleasure that I had. I got away one day to see M. Blondeau, and could only stop with him a moment, because he was very busy; he has not succeeded yet.

You cannot imagine the beauty and magnificence of the Pope's *cortège* and the Emperor's on the coronation day. The Pope went first on his way to Notre Dame. A number of very splendid carriages preceded and followed his, and it put all the others in the shade; it was drawn by eight most beautiful dappled grey horses, their manes covered with plumes that nodded over their heads, and the carriage was as fine as the team. A churchman marched a few paces in front, mounted upon a mule, and bearing a cross; he looked as if he was masquerading, and made the old soldiers, who do not believe in such things, laugh a great deal.

The Emperor passed a few minutes afterwards; he surpassed everyone else. His *cortège* was of the same kind as the

Pope's, but his. carriage much handsomer; his eight dun horses seemed to make it fly majestically. It was all gold, and bore the imperial eagle and crown on the top. More than 80,000 soldiers in new clothing made a line as splendid as it was formidable. What I thought most beautiful was the illumination; everything was on fire, and the blazing lamps were cleverly arranged like trees and designs of every sort. Here was a firework, further on an enormous star, lighting a fountain that flowed with wine.

In a word everything looked heavenly. I should have thought myself in Olympus if I had not been sensible of the miseries of man. I caught a cold the first day of the festivities, and have had it ever since, so that I have endured a great deal, for I could not fall-out; and though it was deathly cold, we had to stick in the mud as upright as posts, and keep on presenting arms. Then there were six miles at least to walk before I could get to bed. I was even obliged to take a carriage back to Fontainebleau, or I could never have got there. Today I have gone into hospital, where we are very comfortable, and I hope I shall soon be better.

Ah, my dear Phillis, how often in these times of suffering did I think La Durantie, my dog, and gun, much better than this silly ambition, that makes a man leave his home to run after fortune through a thousand miseries. How glad I should be to be there with my sisters!

At least they would be sorry for me, and make my illness bearable by their care; instead of which, I am here with strangers who do not even attend to me.

Soon there must be some corporals chosen among us—I hope to be one; that will be one step gained, and I shall be much better off, for-corporal in the Guard ranks with sergeant-major in the Line.

There is an order against our having rooms in town, so I find it almost impossible to do anything till I can get some post that will give me a little room with another man. At this moment we are ten in a room, with only one little table, and as few have any taste for work, it is a witches' Sabbath.

Now comes the first incident in the soldier's life, the transfer of the *vélites* of the guard from Fontainebleau to Courbevoie, and the disappointment at not having been chosen as one of the *vélites* incorporated in the army of Italy. This suburban garrison did not leave our Périgord man any very pleasing remembrances. For the first time he is oppressed and afflicted by disgust.

If I ever come to have done with soldiering, I should be much better pleased to bury myself in the country, than to run after any more adventures. Perhaps the pathetic tone that I adopt makes you think I am weak, and can bear nothing, but if you knew how hard it is to be a soldier for a man who has any spirit, you would think differently.

He returns to his idea of entering the Military School, and meanwhile works at mathematics, and uses his small means in paying a master. The prudent Phillis must have been lecturing her dear brother, as we perceive by one of his letters. These two letters are curious, and show the relaxation of morals at the time.

To his sister Phillis

Fontainebleau, Pluviôse, 1805: I have hardly time to read your letter; I devour it by bits, as I am making up my pack, putting on my sabre, and running to the beat of the drum. Just as I got it, we were told to he ready in an hour, to go to Paris, and on to Italy. We had not a minute, no time to put our things in security, satisfy our creditors, or get our clothes from the wash. We had to go at once, it was four in the afternoon, and tomorrow we have to be by two o'clock in the afternoon at Courbevoie, twenty leagues from Fontainebleau.

Courbevoie, Pluviôse, 1805: We arrived at the appointed time, and four hundred men among us were selected to go to Italy; I was one! But a second order came that only two hundred were to go, and I was not one of them, to my great regret. Those who go are incorporated with the old Grenadiers of the Guard, who are intended for the same destination, and we with those who remain, so that we are now admitted among His Majesty's guards. Thus vanishes my hope of promotion. Now that we are amalgamated with old soldiers, famous not for their science hut for their services, their bravery and their exploits, who nearly all have the cross of merit, it is not to be presumed, and, indeed, it would he unjust, for novices with six months of service ever to command these conquerors of Europe; it is much that we are placed in their ranks. So I was very anxious to go to Italy with the brave fellows, who won their immortality there. I volunteered, but was refused, as I tried a little too late.

I hesitated at first because I had not a halfpenny, had left a few small debts at Fontainebleau, and my properly was by no means secure. I also felt regret at leaving all means of instruction, but when I looked at the condition in which I should find myself at Courbevoie, I did all I could to get away, but to no good.

There were only two hundred men wanted, and all were glad to go. Just now I am in despair at having spoken too late, and am going to lead the most monotonous life here. Courbevoie is a large village, three miles from Paris, where there are no books to fall hack upon, not a master of any kind, and too far from Paris to go and seek instruction in that home of the sciences. I am reduced to spend my days in going on guard, at the Tuileries, in eating and sleeping.

There is nothing to do here, but the universal vice; you can fancy that, at this rate, I do not amuse myself much, and had rather be stupid in my room.

Unprincipled young men are here in a haven of delight. There is hardly a grenadier of the guard who has not a mistress among the laundresses of Paris, who washes for him, feeds him, gives him on Sunday her week's earnings, and is only too happy if he will recompense her by a little fidelity.

It was quite a play, the night before the men marched for Italy, to see a whole company of women, well enough dressed, come to besiege the barrack, and wish their friends goodbye with tears in their eyes. There they were, hanging on their necks, and slipping their little savings of money into their pockets. I know a grenadier to whom a laundress gave fifteen *louis* for his journey.

CHAPTER 4

The Camp at Boulogne (1805)

The Consulate for life had lasted two years. General Bonaparte, who had become First Consul August 2, 1802 (the year X), was proclaimed hereditary Emperor on May 18, 1804 (the year XII), and the people ratified, by 3,572,239 assenting votes, the establishment of the new dynasty. Bugeaud, the *vélite* of the guards, was then twenty. His own station was changed very soon after he had seen his more fortunate companions depart for Italy. This year, 1804, the first of the Empire, was so much disturbed, so fruitful in occurrences, that half-a-century afterwards, the Marshal remembered these events which he had passed through, certainly as a very humble supernumerary, but his observant mind and good sense had formed a sober judgment on them.

It was during the summer of 1805 that the regiment to which Thomas Bugeaud belonged was selected for the camp at Boulogne. The First Consul's immense preparations, and the prodigious activity that he had displayed in his plans for the invasion of England, had been a little disturbed by the grave events of the year 1804, the royalist conspiracy of Georges Cadoudal and Moreau, and the proclamation of the Empire.

An activity, long kept secret, had been developed in our harbours and arsenals. To carry the expeditionary force into England, and attain the object dreamed of by the audacious genius of Napoleon, there was no need for lofty vessels, but for a myriad of gun-boats, flat barges, lighters, and *pinnaces*, propelled by sail and oar; all our ports, even our great inland cities, were put under requisition, and shipyards established all over France. All the master's thoughts had to be swiftly executed. At Paris eighty gun-boats were built on the bank of the Seine, launched and taken to Havre, or sent to other divisions; they were equipped, armed, and sent along the coast towards the Straits of Calais. Squadrons of cavalry and light artillery on shore followed all their movements, ready to protect them against a hostile attack. From the Loire, the Gironde, the Charente, the Adour, all the harbours of the coast issued similar fleets. 1,200 to 1,300 vessels thus collected were to be concentrated at Boulogne, and the neighbouring ports, Wimereux, Etables, and Ambleteuse.

Thomas Bugeaud's pleasant vision of entering the Military School was soon to cease, at the will of the omnipotent Caesar. Indeed, at this period it was perilous enough, or any way very useless, for the subjects of His Majesty, and especially for a *vélite* of the guard, to construct a plan, and build upon tomorrow. The regiment at Courbevoie received orders to march in twenty-four hours for Boulogne-sur-Mer. A letter from Abbeville, dated 16 Messidor, 1805, was written during a halt. In the young soldier's hasty lines there is a sort of breath of patriotism: this is the first, 'We are going on a campaign, and at least the pains we suffer will be useful to the State.'

Is it not in this unconscious feeling of duty, and vision of distant glory, that we find the explanation of the admirable self-denial, discipline, and sublime heroism that Alfred de Vigny has summed up in his valuable work, *Grandeurs et Servitudes Militaires?*

Abbeville, Wednesday, 16 Messidor, 1805: You must have
been astonished at my long silence, but, my dear, you will
not, blame me when your hear that before I answered you, I
was waiting for certainty about a report of our moving, and
that it has been realised. We started for Boulogne six days ago,
and I did not know our actual destination till we came here.
Uncertainty as to when we were going hindered me still further from writing to you. Here I am, my dear, every day trot-
ting out very early, with my pack on my back, and getting
to quarters very tired. I have already-passed through the Isle
of France, and almost all Picardy, a great province, and much
resembling the Limousin in the nature of the soil, but it is
better cultivated. The villages in it are horrible, the houses
no better than our charcoal-burners' huts, and the inhabitants not a bit better-mannered than our boors of Limousins.
Amiens, the capital, celebrated for the famous treaty, seemed
to me commonplace. It would not be worth mentioning
without its cathedral, which is magnificent, and there are
some pretty walks.

At last I am at Abbeville, pleasanter than Amiens. I am
quartered upon a gardener, who seems to be a very good
sort of man; I have been over his garden, and so we talked
of gardening. He told me several little things that I did not
know, and I will give you one of his receipts that may be
useful. If you have a number of lettuces, hearting at the
same time, and wish to keep them in this pleasant condition for a long time, you must carefully pass a knife under
the foot of the plant, and cut the great root that is its centre;
the other little roots will be enough to keep it alive, but
they will not make sap enough to throw up the stalk.

I was working hard to get into the Military School, and
now have to move. But I do not give up this design, as I

can work for it, although at a distance. It is not like me to complain of this last event, as it is for active service. So I say no more, and, though the labour is increased, you shall never see me grumbling, since what. I endure is of use to the State. It is only in garrison that a soldier can complain. I could easily get excused from going, in order to pursue my design, but I would not do the least thing tending that way; it would have been cowardice, otherwise, except as regards my plan, I am delighted to go campaigning.

There is talk of an expedition, and no doubt we shall take part in it; but politicians think it is only to induce the English to make peace. What is certain is, that half of the guard is on the way to the coast, and it is stated that the other half, now on its way from Italy, will come and join us. We have received canvas trousers and frocks for the voyage. We shall be encamped at a short distance from Boulogne. We have a sovereign who will not leave his troops idle, and he has confidence in the *vélites*, for in this expedition we are more numerous than the old grenadiers. As for me, I am quite sure, that, if there is an action, we shall distinguish ourselves, for we are in the best possible spirits, and all delighted to go. In general, in single combat, that is in duels, we are braver than the old grenadiers of the guard. At first they wanted to order us about, but they begin to respect us. In fact, I believe that the Emperor thinks much more of us than he does of them, and that one day or other the *vélites* will form a separate body.

> The detachment to which Thomas Bugeaud belonged was ordered to proceed to the camp at Wimereux, and he then wrote the following letter to his sister, giving an account of several engagements with the English vessels cruising off our coasts, in order to distract our labours, and oppose the concentration of our little flotillas at Boulogne.

Wimereux, near Boulogne, 1805: I arrived, my dear Phillis, at the camp of Wimereux, near Boulogne, in very good health, and was very much interested in examining all these things, new to me: a very large camp, harbours, flotillas, the sea; the sight of all this gives me the greatest pleasure. Our camp, not a musket-shot from the sea, is very pretty, at a distance, it would be taken for a beautiful village. In truth, it is not very comfortable, as we have to lie on a little straw, the bed is by no means good, but one is not so badly off here as I expected. Now, also, I am used to it, and it is not physical privation or fatigue that troubles me. Three days after my arrival, a detachment was embarked, of whom I was one. We were eleven days at sea, and you would not suspect that in this time I have been present at three naval engagements, two of them sharp enough. You should see the account in the papers, but I think that some particulars will be of interest to you, when you know I was there.

As we went out, the English came to attack us with several frigates, brigs, and corvettes; we were rather surprised, for we did not expect to fight, and hardly any of the crew had ever seen the sea. We knew no sea terms for the management of the sails, or gun drill for firing the cannon; but we had to perform both duties, both quite strange to us. When we were told to let go a rope, we hauled upon it as hard as we could, and this at first caused some confusion, and took us nearer to the enemy than we wished. However, in a short time, we got used to our work, and we kept up a smart fire with the help of the forts and coast batteries; the enemy were compelled to haul off, and we got quit of them for some slight damage.

Two shots came on board the gunboat where I was without doing much harm. After this skirmish we anchored in the roads, and stayed there pretty quietly for some days; I was only sea-sick for a quarter of an hour.

In the quiet days we were practised in manoeuvring, and lost no time in putting our theory into practice, for there was a signal that a flotilla was coming from Calais; and either to make a diversion, or to protect it, we made ready at daybreak. The English soon perceived that we were in motion, and attacked us furiously; we received them just the same way, and the combat was sharp enough for an hour and a half; the enemy were again obliged to haul off, and it is said were considerably damaged. On our side we were very fortunate, for there were only three or four men wounded, some masts cut, and other injuries, slight enough. In our gunboat there was only one shot that went through from starboard to port, and killed no one. The Dutch fleet was not as fortunate; all the way from Dunkirk here it had to keep up a fight with forty-seven sails, three or four of them being line-of-battle ships; in the evening it came in sight, continually harassed by the English, and keeping up a vigorous defence.* Some of our line were engaged, but it did not last long, as the enemy suffered severely from the batteries and forts on the coast. The Dutch had eighty men killed or wounded. It is time, my dear, to finish this gazette, which may weary you, but it amuses me to write it.

Napoleon had invented several methods for keeping the enemy at a distance. He established several lines of submarine batteries, armed with heavy guns, covered by high tide, and uncovered at low water, so that the fire seemed to advance and retire with the tide itself. Five hundred pieces

---

* English vessels at Wimereux, *Immortalité*, frigate; *Hebe*, 32 guns; *Arab*, 20 guns; and the remainder of the detached squadron. Only damage, a nine-pounder gun disabled.'—*James' Naval History*, vol. iii. p. 311. See also pp. 312 and 313 for Action with Dunkirk Flotilla. Only small vessels were suitable for the service, on account of shoal-water.

of the largest calibre were placed in battery upon the reefs the English call 'the iron coast,' and forts built out at sea prevented the enemy's approach to the harbour. Several of these batteries fired hollow projectiles.

Everything was ready, only waiting for a fair wind und favourable weather. The English had recourse to their usual plan of organizing a confederation. Admiral La Touche Treville died; Villeneuve, who succeeded him, did not carry out the plans with sufficient dash. The Emperor began by abusing Austria and Villeneuve.

The violence and injustice of the Emperor's expressions vexed Admiral Decrès. 'Villeneuve is a wretch who must be dismissed with ignominy,' cried he; 'he has no power of combination, no courage, nor general energy, he would lose everything to save his skin.'

He was raging thus in the presence of Monge, for whom he had a real friendship, notwithstanding the known opinions of the savant, who had remained a republican. Annoyed at Napoleon's rage, Monge went and told M. Daru, first secretary for war. Daru went to the Emperor. Misinformed as to his master's intentions, and the cause of his displeasure, he waited in silence; the Emperor came to him, and cried, 'Do you know where Villeneuve is? At Cadiz!' And detailing to M. Daru all the plans he had been hatching for six months, attributing their failure to the cowardice and incapacity of the men he had employed, he broke out into invectives and abuse. All at once, as if he had eased his soul by this outburst of passion, he said to M. Daru, 'Sit down and write.'

A powerful effort, and the natural play of a fertile imagination, says M. Guizot, had caused him to revert to the combinations that were to make his enemies tremble, and ensure him over Austria the triumph which he had missed over England. The plan of his campaign was arranged; all his thoughts turned to execute his will like lightning.

CHAPTER 5

Austerlitz (1805)

Our land forces were now to find themselves in their real element; and very soon great excitement was to ensue after the abortive enterprise of the camp at Boulogne. The capitulation of Ulm, the battle of Austerlitz, the reconstruction of Austria, were destined in this same year to announce to Europe the accession of a new Emperor. By some of the continual chances of war our young soldier was only a spectator of this grand drama until the day of Austerlitz. He writes to his sister from Saint Quentin that after the daily alarms, embarkation and disembarkation at Boulogne, the march was as pleasant as travelling; after an hour's rest he used to go and see anything curious in the town where they halted. Another letter:

To his sister Phillis

Augsburg, 18 Vendémiaire, 1805: I only rested one day at Strasburg; we crossed the Rhine, and made forced marches that have wearied us very much. We move off very early every day, and do not stop till night. All the army marches as sharply, and our *little man* drives the ship with astonishing speed. Good feet are wanted to second the activity of his mind. You can judge of the speed of our march when you know that we have gone eighty leagues in a week, a

great deal for loaded troops; for besides our packs we carry
on our backs all our campaigning kit—kettles, canteens,
picks, spades, &c.

I am absolutely tired out, and cannot imagine how the
body can support such constant fatigue. Again, if we had
but a good bed when we get to our quarters; but not a bit
of it, we only have a little straw, and even that after three
or four hours' delay, and often we can only lie in the open
round a fire. Hunger is another tyrant. You can imagine
whether ten thousand men coming into a village can easily find anything to eat. What distresses me more is the
annoyance of stealing from the peasantry; their poultry,
their bacon, their firewood, taken from them by grace or
force. I do not do these things, but when I am very hungry I secretly tolerate them, and eat my share of the stolen
goods. All this plainly shows that hitherto I have only seen
the rosy side.

But do not suppose that I am wanting in strength and
courage to bear these evils, though I do seem to express
disgust. On the contrary, I endure them with patience, and
try to fill my place honourably. I assure you I will die or
distinguish myself. I am most anxious to win the cross of
merit; and only want an opportunity.

There has been fighting already, and we had the best of
it. On the 16th four thousand prisoners were taken, whom
I have seen march by; there were several officers of good
appearance, many of them covered with blood. It is stated
that General Murat has blocked eleven thousand more men
three leagues off, and that we shall march tomorrow to
compel them to surrender more speedily.

Do not be surprised if I am a long time without writing
to you, perhaps two months.

6 November

Linz, in Austria, 16 Brumaire, 1805: Till now, my dear, I have had no time to tell you anything about the campaign we are making, or rather have already made, for the Emperor allows us to count it as a campaign already on account of our brilliant success. I have hardly had breathing time; we have been always on the run, either to cut off the enemy, or to pursue him; I take advantage of a little rest to entertain myself with you, and to describe at large the various actions and operations that have taken place.

After Strasburg we made long marches, crossing the principality of Baden, and the electorate of Wurtemburg, then entered into Swabia. The enemy fled before us; the first affairs took place near Augsburg, where we made five or six thousand prisoners. Several small affairs, that took place before the capture of Ulm, were always to our advantage, but it was at Ulm that we secured a complete success by the quick and skilful manoeuvres of the French army. The enemy found themselves divided and were obliged to surrender; I have had the pleasure of seeing twenty-eight thousand men march past, who had laid down their arms. It was a fine sight.

The army was arranged semi-circularly in *échelon* on a low hill that surrounds Ulm; the Emperor was on a rock, near which we were formed up, he was surrounded by the principal generals of the army, and watched the enemy's army pass, as it were at his feet, coming out of one of the gates of the city, and going in at another after laying down their arms. He watched it all with a quiet and modest glance, warming himself by a fire we had lighted for him, where by the way he burnt the grey riding-coat that he seems to regard rather superstitiously. After seeing the enemy parade in this beautiful way, we reversed and turned

back to Augsburg, where we made but a short stay, for the
Emperor will take no rest until he has entirely conquered
his enemy.

We crossed Bavaria, entirely cleared of Austrians by our
advanced guard, and rested two days at Munich, the capital.
It is a fair city, but offers none of the conveniences or pleasures that are to be found in our French towns. The enemy
were entrenched on the banks of the Inn, the river that
divides Austria and Bavaria. They were driven off without
difficulty, and we have marched here as easy as travelling,
except for some little skirmishes.

On the route we saw occasionally places where there
had been a little fighting. Only some five or six Russians
were to be seen on the field of battle; no French at all, no
doubt they had been buried.

Just as I am writing to you, two thousand prisoners have
reached this town, Austrians and Russians in equal numbers, taken yesterday and the day before. The fighting was
sharp, and the advantage all on our side. Report says that
our camp is twenty-five leagues from here, and that we are
only forty-eight post leagues from Vienna. I fully believe
that, if they do not come to terms, we shall soon see that
famous capital, for the enemy seem in no condition to resist us; they defend themselves so badly that we are nearly
sure to beat them.

No doubt you suppose that, with such a quantity of success, I have been often in action, and my life twenty times
in danger. Well, not in the least, my dear; I have hardly run
any risk, our corps has not been engaged yet, and this is unfortunate. There is nothing to hope for, as perhaps we shall
not be in action at all this whole campaign; and then no
promotion! In war it is not the fighting that is to be feared;
on the contrary, it is often wished for as a deliverance from
the sufferings, weariness, and privations that are more cruel

than death. I can assure you that one day, when we were in front of the enemy, that is to say, in the second line, hut very near, it rained, snowed, and hailed by turns, and I twenty times wished they would let us charge. We were obliged to remain in the ranks, carrying our packs, unable to light a fire, with nothing to eat, having had no bread for four or five days, wet to the bones; and that went on all day and part of the night, till we took possession of a very strong village that the enemy had held.

I was weak enough that day to wish for death, and longed for one of the shot that I saw rush through our ranks. If we had received the order to charge at such a time, we should certainly have put everything to death. I do not tell you of the horrors of war, the villages sacked, the wrongs and barbarities that it brings in its train. I keep such tales for the happy time when we shall meet again. Now I will only tell you that the profession of a hero is so much like that of a brigand that I hate it with my whole soul. A man must have a heart of stone, destitute of all humanity, to love war.

To his sister Phillis

Brunnen, 4 Frimaire, 1805: You did not expect, my love, that my first letter would be written from forty leagues beyond Vienna, that is to say, from the capital of Moravia. I wanted to write to you from the proud capital that we have just humbled, but we only passed through it. I hardly saw enough to tell you anything about it, but I must say something, or you will tell me I do not know how to notice anything.

Vienna is situated in a very small plain; the neighbourhood is very populous, and the villages so many and so beautiful that the whole plain might be taken for one immense city. But the pleasure houses that these villages are composed of are not adorned with the beauties of nature, as

50

is the case at Paris. There are no charming English gardens to be seen, no groves, no hedgerow elms, and labyrinths such as form the charm of these sort of dwellings. The houses are quite bare, with only some trees giving a little shade. Approaching the city on the side towards France, there is a great suburb, handsomer than any at Paris. At the end of this suburb is an open space, at the end of which stands the Emperor's palace, close to the gate of the city. The inside is very mean, there is no ornament about it, and I venture to say that the court is not twice as large as that at La Durantie. On the other hand, it is said that the apartments are of unrivalled magnificence.

As for me, the only fine thing I saw was a pair of colossal statues at one of the gates. The rest of the city presented nothing of interest; but the houses are almost all well built. What surprised me was the confidence prevailing everywhere in the city; the shops were open, ladies, even the most elegant, passed among the French soldiers in the streets, and the faces were as calm as if we had been in the depths of peace.

Oh, my dear Phillis, how my heart bled when I saw that we passed this city by, when the capture of it seemed as if it ought to be the limit of our labours and miseries. I conjured up a very lamentable picture of my future lot; I already attributed Alexander's ambition to our Emperor, and imagined myself one of the old Macedonians, whom he dragged about the world, and who sighed unceasingly for their families and country.

By way of consolation, we marched the whole night, and in three days have made forty and some odd leagues. On the march we saw a place where there had been a fight. Joseph Debetz was in action there; and I was in fear for his life when I saw a number of dead, both French and Russians I looked at the buttons, and saw several of the 75th, his regiment, among the killed. I passed on thinking our friend dead, for I had been told that a great many officers were killed; but in a village near I found a soldier of his corps, who told me he was well, and he afterwards sent me his compliments.

At last the Emperor has restrained his thunders, to our great astonishment; for we are halted in this town, without much idea of the reason, for, though we are in the middle of everything that goes on, our ignorance is complete, and we are real machines. The inaction of the troops makes me hope that perhaps a treaty is just being made. It is even stated that we shall soon go back to Vienna.

The day when I turn my steps backwards towards my beloved France will be a joyful one for me. No longer will the days' marches seem long to me when every step is bringing me nearer to my family, and especially to my dear sisters. I have always been very well, but a heavy cold has caught hold of me here. This is a fine way to cure it; we are always under arms, being reviewed, or inspected; indeed, we have a little too much tyranny; after a march of five hundred leagues, we are obliged to be as well turned out as at Paris, and if we fall short on the smallest point we are punished or reprimanded as if for a capital crime.

To his sister Phillis

Brunnen, the Capital of Moravia, 19 Frimaire, 1805: Do not be surprised at my silence, my dear, the speed of our march, and the little rest we have had, have given me no chance of writing to you lately; but to-day I shall make myself a little compensation.

An illness of the Emperor delays us in this village for two or three days, and this gives me a moment to communicate with you. As I know you are curious to hear all particulars, I will resume my account of the campaign from Augsburg.

After my return from Ulm, we left that city, and made our way straight to Munich, the capital of Bavaria, and rested there three days. We then crossed the rest of Bavaria to march against the Russians, who were upon the banks of the Inn. The enemy kept on retreating, and as far as Vienna there were only some slight affairs with their rear-guard. So we crossed Austria like travellers, and after a halt of three days at Lentz, we reached that proud capital, and its capture seemed to be the limit of our labours and miseries; but, alas, my dear, what was my surprise and grief when I saw that we were crossing the city without a halt!

At a short distance from Vienna a large number of prisoners were taken, and a large park of artillery captured. Next day we reached the scene of a very sharp conflict with the Russians which had just taken place; the dead covered the plain on both sides of the road. I looked at some of them to see the different regiments that had been engaged; and saw several of the 75th. I inquire and am told that this regiment had suffered considerably and lost a number of officers; but learnt, at last, that Joseph is well, and got off with a few knocks on the head.

We entered Moravia and have stayed some days in the capital, where I still am. There is talk of peace; ambassadors have come, but no doubt the conditions have seemed too harsh to them. The enemy preferred to try the hazard of a battle, they concentrated their forces at a distance of four leagues from here; their army was formidable, and the two Emperors commanded in person.

Three days before the battle we had orders to leave the town, and encamped a league from the enemy. The Emperor came there himself and slept in his carriage in the middle of our camp. For the three days that passed before the battle he was always walking through all the camps, and talking to the soldiers or their leaders.

We gathered round him. I heard much of his talk; it was very simple and always turned upon military duty. At last, on the eve of the battle, the anniversary of his coronation, he issued a proclamation exhorting us to behave with our usual intrepidity, and promised to keep his distance as long as victory followed us. 'But,' said he, 'if by mischance you hesitate a moment, you will see me fly into your ranks to restore order.' Then he promised to give us peace after this battle, assuring us that we should go into cantonments.

We replied by shouts of joy, the harbingers of glad success. Torches were lighted and the bands played while the whole army sang songs with eagerness. It seemed that every man was celebrating his return home, and felt the joy one experiences at seeing father, mother, and brother. Yet how many of these happy men were not to see their country again?

At daybreak the drums and trumpets announced the fight; a start was made with shouts of *'Vive l'Empereur.'* The charge is sounding. These words are repeated again louder, and carry terror into the enemy's ranks. We charged like lightning, and the carnage was horrible. The balls whistled. The air groaned with the noise of cannon and our threatening voices, closely followed by death. Very soon the enemy's phalanx was shaken and thrown into disorder, at last we overthrew them entirely. One point withstands us, the batteries in a moment are taken, the gunners cut to pieces at their guns, and any that escape our steel either seek safety in flight, or a slower death in the lakes.

Nothing has ever been seen, my love, like this memorable battle. In the opinion of the oldest soldiers it is the most bloody that has ever taken place. I will not describe to you the horrors of the field of battle; the wounded and dying imploring their comrades' pity. I prefer to spare your feelings, and confine myself to telling you that I was very much affected, and wished that emperors and kings who make war without reasonable grounds could be condemned for their whole lives to listen to the cries of the unfortunate wounded, who remained three days upon the field of battle without having any relief or assistance.

The Russian loss is innumerable; what is certain is that there are to be seen at least sixty Russian corpses on the field of battle for one French; and it is only in one spot that I have seen nearly as many French as Russians.

Since that day there has been no more fighting. The two Emperors met in our presence; it is stated that the German promised whatever the French one chose to demand. The troops are retiring; we return to Vienna tomorrow, and I hope we shall not be long before we take the road to Paris. When we get there I shall ask for leave, and fly home. It is by your side, close to all of you, that I hope to get a recompense for all my fatigues, and to forget my troubles. One moment will blot everything out, as I embrace you with a full heart.

The Emperor has made a little harangue in a proclamation that has been read throughout the army. It expresses his approbation of our bravery, and commences with these words—'Soldiers, I am satisfied with you.' Then he promises us a peace worthy of us, and announces our speedy return to our own country, and the joy of our countrymen at seeing us. The speech winds up—'It will be enough for you to say, "I was at the battle of Austerlitz," for men to exclaim—"Here is a brave man!"'

In reading these letters of an obscure *vélite*, do we not seem to hear the whole Grand Army revealing its inmost thoughts to the world, imbued by turns with a sadness verging on despair, or an enthusiasm reaching to superstition? We have only to observe in what cities these fraternal outpourings are written. At this simple enumeration of capitals do we not see the great shadow of the modern

Caesar depriving the ancient House of Hapsburg of its German electorates and Slav kingdoms, tearing the imperial crown of the West from the only heir of Rudolph, refashioning the world with blows of an axe, to borrow a celebrated expression?

What an almost supernatural effect must this man have produced upon the generations born to contemplate him, or to feed his glory! And yet how many obscure heroes dragged in his train begged for mercy from the future prisoner of Saint Helena, seeing, like Alexander's Macedonians, in every river the extreme boundary of their conquests, every important city the aim of their labours!

Having achieved his two corporal's stripes upon the field of Austerlitz, the future Marshal of France, who carried the golden baton—dotted with bees—in his pack, was sent back to France. It was from Courbevoie, the depot of the Imperial Guard, that he sends this good news to his sister, the 26th of February, 1806. The date of his letters is no longer in Republican terms. His glorious master had abolished the traces of the Revolution.

TO HIS SISTER PHILLIS

Courbevoie, 26 February, 1806: At last, my dear, here I am back in Paris.

On arriving I found, as expected, my promotion as corporal in the guard. My captain informed me, and the proof's of his good opinion that he gave me are the first pleasures I have had in my new profession. He told me that he was very sorry that he could not get me made quartermaster-sergeant, that he did all he could, but that, unfortunately, other young men had better interest than his could be, and that was the only thing that stood in my way. 'Besides,' he said, 'you ought to be satisfied with the rank of corporal; it is more important than you suppose, and may carry you a long way, especially as you gained it in a campaign. A man must go through it to go further; one step more, and you are a sub-lieutenant in the line.'

I await this step, my love, with much impatience, because it will give me the means to recover my liberty if I choose, and by that means draw near to you. At this moment I am compelled by prudence to abstain from such a pleasant meeting. You know, and you have often told me, that it is necessary to consider the future, 'that a man must not sacrifice the interests of his forty years to the wishes of the moment, and that it is wise to draw back for a better leap.'

Well, my dear, that is what I wish to do. It is to our friendship, which will, I hope, last more than forty years, that I sacrifice the pleasure of meeting you; but if I can gain the epaulette, no further ambition will be able to stop me. I shall fly to you, to you all, and doubly rejoice, for I shall have in some measure gained the liberty of resting at home, if my taste does not incline to soldiering. It would be impossible to get leave at this moment. I am attached to the new corps of *vélites*, and their instruction absolutely requires the presence of all the non-commissioned officers.

On the 6th of April, 1806, two months afterwards, Thomas announced to Phillis, from Paris, his appointment as sub-lieutenant in the 64th Regiment of the Line. Corporal of the Guard then was an equivalent rank to sergeant-major in the Line. He now has his epaulette, and says, 'When I think that I have at last escaped from the miseries, it seems to me that it is a dream, and a very agreeable dream.'

To his sister Phillis

Paris, 6 April, 1806: You had, my dear, a great idea of my deserts when I told you that I was corporal. What would you think now if you knew that I am a sub-lieutenant? When I come to think that I am at last escaped from the unpleasantness of the military profession, it seems to me that it is a dream, and a very agreeable dream. When I was positively told of my new appointment, I wanted to tell you all about my new regiment, and that has delayed me; for I do not know yet what I shall be appointed to, and have a great notion I shall not receive my commission till the *fête*. I suppose I am not on the active list, for it is said that most of those who, like me, have been made sub-lieutenants will be at the heels of the regiments. So I have taken steps to avoid being one of them, and have obtained a formal promise to be placed upon the active list. I have had the good fortune in all this to be in the company of a captain, with whom I was in two or three engagements at Boulogne, and who thought he saw some courage in me. Added to this regular conduct I have a little dexterity in making myself useful in moments of difficulty, and these are the causes of my promotion.

I count with great impatience the moments that divide me from a leave that must be granted.

But there soon came disenchantments to cool this charming delight. After a stay at Besançon, he was again sent into Germany. It is true the Emperor had no railways; but his valiant troops skipped from north to south, without a thought of danger or fatigue. A letter dated from Waldhausen, in Franconia, August 6, 1806, shows us the lieutenant face to face with a surly colonel. From that time he becomes melancholy. 'Yes, my dear, I shall leave off soldiering as soon as we have a Continental peace. Every day I confirm myself in this resolution. The future has to be considered, for I see plainly that this is not a profession for life.'

Besançon, July 9, 1806: No doubt, my dear, you believe that I am far away in Germany. Well! I am still in France, and this is the way. The depot of my regiment is at Besançon; and as that town was on my road, I went to pay my respects to the major commanding it. He has kept me here as he wants officers, and the battalions at the front have their full number.

The town is charming, but I have little time to enjoy it. I work hard at all that an officer cannot get on without knowing. First at drill, then again at the financial administration of corps, and military law. All this will not allow me a moment, because I do not choose to be ignorant of anything that makes a well-informed soldier, and can only be learnt by study or long practice.

The fat major is very good to me. He is lively, speaks kindly, and is really the most amiable of superior officers. He has confidence enough in me to give me the command of a company, which has no other officers.

My journey here has been very pleasant; I always travelled with pretty women, or sensible men, across beautiful country. Moulins and Lyons are the finest towns I have seen, but Lyons is especially magnificent, not so much by buildings as by the peculiarity of its position. On one side, the town lies against some very fertile hills, on the other side is a vast and fruitful plain. The Rhone traverses it, and surrounds it on the eastern side, then joins the Saône, a little below, so that a portion of the city is on an island. Though this city is very populous, it is dull at this moment, for trade is annihilated.

I hope you have been told the reasons that prevented my going to Bordeaux; in truth, the expense of my outfit had put me much in arrear. When leaving Paris, I examined my purse to see if it would take me to Bordeaux; but I found with pain that it would only just take me to La Durantie. When I got there, I found a very hearty welcome, but very little money. So on my departure, I only asked for ten *louis*; but Patrice made me a present of a mare which I sold on the way, and that was a great help to me.

To his sister Phillis

Besançon, July 19, 1806: How confused I am! Perhaps you may not believe it, but I thought I had answered you. My affection suggested some doubts, and thinking carefully, I found that I was in arrear. This forgetfulness may surprise you, but your astonishment will cease, when you think that, as my thoughts always run upon you, I fancy I have written what I only thought. I have to make a calculation in order to remember, because I have several ways of communicating with you; that by letter is too dry; my ideas are shut-in by certain rules, that deprive them of expression. But when I walk alone it is very different. Then I give free course to my feelings. They jostle, overturn, and mount upon each other; then, without consulting me, fly like an arrow off to Bordeaux. Your brother is a little mad with his castles in the air, but at those times he deserves your friendship, for he always put you in the best place.

Since I have joined, I have spent a very active life of it. I have no time for mischief; I am doing the duty of adjutant-major, and this puts on me the drill as well as the police of the whole battalion. Perhaps you will not be sorry to know how my time is employed. This is it: drill from five in the morning till seven; from seven to nine study in my room; at nine I parade the sergeant-majors, and take them to the major in command, to receive his orders for duty; at ten I have all the non-commissioned officers, and instruct them in the theory and practice of soldiering; at half-past eleven

I inspect the men for guard; from noon till three I am tolerably free, but I have the interior administration of a company, and that takes up some of this time. At three I go to dinner; then to the *café*, to read the papers. This brings me to five o'clock, when drill begins again and lasts till seven. After that I go for a stroll or pay some visits, and come back to my room to work till eleven. Add to all this bustle four or five changes of clothes in the day, and you can fancy if I have any time to rest. The post of adjutant-major is hard, but I would be glad to take it, because I should have the rank of captain, and that gives some prominence where the work is well done.

To his sister Phillis

Waldhausen, in Franconia, August 6, 1806: I only received your letter after my return to the Grand Army. It arrived in the nick of time, for I was tired to death.

Two days before I had been sent to a lonely village to command a detachment; I had not become used to my rude habitation, and wanted something pleasant to restore me to my usual happy state. For I am quite in hopes that you will now change your opinion, and that you will have made out an explanation of the causes that prevented my journey to Bordeaux.

Duty laid a strict injunction on me to join at once, and political news also hastened my departure. A war with the North was reported; my regiment lay in that direction, and I had every reason to expect that it would be on the march before I could reach it. It would have cost me a great deal of money to follow it alone, and I might have had the pain of hearing that it had come in contact with the enemy before my arrival. These I think are valid reasons enough, but they are not all; when I got to La Durantie, I found I had not a penny, and the little money I could get to meet the cost of a long journey would not allow me to visit you. I thought it was wiser to go at once to the regiment, and ask for leave when my savings will allow of my making this much-desired journey.

I think I told you of the kindness of the major (the second personage of the regiment), and the good reception he gave me. Well, my dear, the colonel's was as bad as his was good. He has a very harsh manner, and always seems as if he had a spite against one. He hardly said four words to me, and his first were, 'You have been expected a long time, sir.'

I made haste to ask his commands, so as to quit him the more quickly, determining not to go and see him very often. If I intended to continue my military career, I would manage to find a way to get into his good graces; but as I reckon upon abandoning the profession altogether, I will not take any trouble about it.

Yes, my dear, I shall leave off soldiering as soon as we have a Continental peace. Every day do I fortify myself more and more in this intention. The future has to be considered, and I see plainly that this is not a profession for life. I allow that an officer finds a good many pleasant things in it; but it is only good during youth, and men often find themselves in very unpleasant positions. The devil must be taken by the tail, to provide the turn-out that is required, and a man often runs the risk of spending all his fortune; and I should do this certainly if I remained, as the way to attract notice is to make a display. Then, if one has the misfortune to displease the chief of the corps, he compels one by main force to send in one's papers, and in a moment you lose ten years' service. Every day do I see officers in this case. That alone would be enough to make me retire, and I do not wish to expose myself to loss of years which I might employ to greater advantage. Just now I have gained more than lost, having travelled much, seen the world, and have not devoured my little portion.

My travel into Germany was most easy. I always had a carriage-and-four which cost me nothing, and I was glad to offer a place to ladies going the same way. At this moment I only need pride and fierceness to be like the *seigneurs* of old limes; for I really have a barony under my orders. I have five villages under my command, occupied by my detachment. I have only to speak, and I am instantly obeyed. Yet, with all these advantages, I find it very dull; I have no society but that of the peasants, and no books.

You will oblige me, my dear, by giving me your advice as to my desire to leave the service. When you give it me, observe that in the present state of things there cannot be any more speedy promotion, as there was in the time of the Revolution. Four years must be spent as sub-lieutenant to qualify for lieutenant, as many for the rank of captain, and so on. I tell you plainly, the miseries of war, the pillage, the vexations, the cruelties, the ruin of the inhabitants, often make me detest my profession. It only pleases me when I think of glory, and the great men who have made themselves famous. But that is a gust of wind that is soon passed.

The poor inhabitants must be entirely ruined. All devour them, from the private to the General in command. There are Generals who give entertainments and banquets which cost as much as 600 *florins* (1,350 francs), and all at the cost of the people. Keep this to yourself. I assure you that I spend nothing but what I am obliged, and that the innkeeper benefits by me.

Chapter 6.

Poland (1806)

The Treaty of Presburg was signed, and Napoleon organized the Confederation of the Rhine on the ruins of the German Empire. Europe might expect a peace. But the interlude had hardly begun when it was almost, over. There was to be no rest at this period.

Less than a year after the battle of the three Emperors Prussia attempted to eclipse Austria on pretence of revenging her. A rash idea, destined to be dissipated by more disgraceful and more really decisive reverses than had befallen her rival. The battles of Jena and Auerstadt, the capitulation of Erfurth, and some actions now forgotten, delivered the kingdom of the Hohenzollerns to Bonaparte.

Like the descendants of Maria Theresa, the heirs of the great Frederick begged for Russian support, and Napoleon found his old Moravian opponents in the steppes of Poland. Sub-lieutenant Bugeaud performed this new triumphal march in the French army, and gained a bitter remembrance of it to carry with him all the days of his life, for the day of Pultusk brought him his first wound, as that of Austerlitz had beheld the winning of his first stripes.

To his sister Phillis

Warsaw, 29 December, 1806: I have been wishing to write to you, my dear, for the last four or five days, but I had hardly begun when a sudden order came to go in pursuit of the Russians. The drum beat, we made a start, and having left Warsaw, we passed in succession the Vistula and the Bug, at a distance of about seven leagues.

During the night we had carried the enemy's entrenchments at the point, of the bayonet, and driven him towards the Neva, It was on the24th that this took place; on the 25th there was only a small cavalry skirmish; but on the 26th an army corps found itself placed before the enemy in a little plain near the Neva. We were very inferior in numbers, for our forces had not all come up, among them the artillery, as the roads were so bad. However, there was no hesitation to attack, for we are always used to conquer.

The chief part of our force was posted on the left, for the enemy threatened to outflank us on that side, thanks to a wood that covered them. On our right we had only three battalions of our brigade, unsupported by any cavalry. With this handful of men we attacked a great line of infantry, protected by several batteries, and supported by a large force of cavalry. Our impetuosity threw them into disorder; they fled on all sides, and the guns would have been in our possession if the deep mud had not prevented our moving speedily. A man could hardly drag his legs out of it. At this moment the cavalry charged our left, which had no time to form, because all the men were stuck in the mud, and could only move very slowly.

Notwithstanding their terrible fire, the two battalions on the left were overthrown and driven upon the first, where I was. Happily we had time to form square, but we were afraid we should be thrown into disorder by our own comrades in their attempt to escape from death, and we were compelled to kill a good many of them to save the rest, because they were between us and the cavalry. We waited till the mass was within twenty paces of us. Suddenly a fearful discharge confounded and stopped the horsemen—they fell like hail; the rest were seized with a panic, and a shameful flight deprived them of the small share of glory they owed only to the dreadful slate of the ground.

During our short reverse the enemy's gunners had bravely returned to their pieces, and their infantry had rallied. So we had to encounter a much superior fire. We bore it well, and when we had fired all our cartridges, the officers collected any they could from the killed, and gave them to the men.

Hitherto I had been lucky, but a ball came, and struck me just above the left knee. A soldier came and took me by the arm to lead me to the ambulance; but when he had gone a few paces my conductor was killed by a bullet. So I was left alone in the mud, and, to add to my misfortunes, some fresh squadrons of cavalry came by the rear of our square, and passed just where I was. I had no resource but to feign death; and they were no more successful in this charge than the first. A man picked me up, and led me to a village, where my wound was dressed.

To make the scene more tragic, the house where I was caught fire. I dragged myself as best I could to another quarter, and from there was carried to Warsaw, where I now am pretty comfortable. My only fear is that I shall never be able to march comfortably, for the tendon is touched. I never rightly knew how the action ended, but think it was to the advantage of the French.

I have told you my misfortunes—now to cheer you up I will tell you my good luck. I was made a lieutenant a week ago by the Emperor at a review he held here. This is consolation!

> The following letter, also from Warsaw, mentions the wound; it led to no bad consequences. A certain difficulty in some movements was the only thing that in future reminded the Marshal of this almost inevitable consequence

of the profession of arms. As for his horror at the ruined villages, the plains strewed with corpses, the wounded left without help, the fruitless appeals addressed by the living to their friends of the day before, whom they were never to see again, the wars in Spain, France, and Africa, will show how far the new-made officer was cured. Again, how many mighty men of war have been affected like the heroine of Domremy by the first action, who were destined afterwards to sacrifice whole generations with the carelessness of Catherine the Great!

In this letter the young officer's tone is curiously changed. We find him a very civilised man of the world, and we would wager that his enforced detention at Warsaw—that Capua of the North—went a long way in the change effected. Certainly the society of the Polish ladies, those enchantresses, very much aroused the animation and wit of the young Frenchman, who sometimes seems to us somewhat worldly-wise and experienced for a young officer of twenty-two.

To his sister Phillis

Warsaw, 21 February, 1807: Be comforted, my dear, I am not crippled! I shall be able to march easily, but perhaps shall never be quite so strong for forced marches; for this, added to a sprain I have had, gives me but a poor leg. I was almost entirely cured by the time of the Carnival, but having chosen to go out too soon, and even having spent the night at a masked ball, my wound broke out bleeding again, and I was as bad as before for a few days. Now it is getting much better, and I hope that in a few days I shall be in condition to rejoin my corps.

I fancy I hear you saying, 'He is always the same giddy fellow; he will never change!' Perhaps you are right. However, if I went out too soon, it was because I was very anxious to join my regiment, and had to walk about to get used to severe marches . . . .

I am quartered upon a miniature-painter, who is much thought of; and it makes his house very agreeable that he and his children are very good musicians. Though still very young, they speak six or seven languages, among them French, with considerable purity.

I am absolutely in the midst of the arts and sciences. I never felt before what it is to have no talents; I think of it, every moment. Why was I born in a cursed country where the arts and sciences are almost ignored?

In this country they are very much tainted with nobility. The gentlemen are unbearably proud, especially towards their own peasants, who never approach them without kissing their feet, or making a show of doing it. They were very much surprised that the French took no more account, of a palatine, or gentleman, than of any other burgess. As we do not know how to bow our heads to the ground, we have been considered unmannerly.

Lately, two ladies were rather stupidly telling stories of French incivility before me. One said, 'Today an officer very rudely asked me to show him where his quarters were.' The other said, 'Madam, this is much worse. Two officers all over mud were quartered upon me the other day. They were shown into my apartments; I went out to give some orders, and these gentlemen, thinking themselves at home, changed their boots and shirts—in a word, made their whole *toilette.*'

I instantly thought of revenge, as this feeling is natural to us; and fancied that the best way was to vindicate the French women. 'Ladies,' said I, 'we are trained in camps, and it is not surprising that our manners sometimes partake of the roughness of our employment. But if you knew the ladies of France, you would judge much better of the nation. They are polite and modest, they have the tone of good society, and especially much fairness and kindness; never do they utter in conversation the smallest word that could annoy anyone. They are dainty, and display a multitude of little attentions that charm everyone, even the persons who at first thought themselves neglected. They are virtuous, but no prudes; on the contrary, gaiety and enjoyment are their most graceful attributes. In a word, ladies, they have in general all the amiable and solid qualities that a reasonable man, a fool, a giddy-pate, or a philosopher could desire. Oh, my dear country, when shall I revisit you?'

I saw my two Poles blush and bite their lips, but neither said a word. I was silent, and saw that the portrait of my country-women I had drawn had gained me a little consideration.

They no doubt thought that a man who was able to see so many qualities in their sex, could not fail to perceive those that were wanting in them.

I think, my love, I have chattered enough for today; yet I do not choose to go to bed before assuring you that I am the most tender of brothers,

> When cured of his wound, Lieutenant Bugeaud had to return to France, to the depot of his regiment at Be-sançon. He passed through Berlin, and stayed there some time. His observations are short, but effective. He writes: 'We are really esteemed in this country, as much on account of our success as for our freedom from pride. They compare us with their own officers, who were vain and insolent; they got no advantage from it. Alas, their pride is much abased.'

To his sister Phillis

Besançon, May 28, 1807: After a journey divided between storms and pleasures, I happily reached Besançon, where one of your good long letters was already awaiting me. Thank you for your advice, always good and prudent, though it is only founded upon your simple judgment.

It will please you much that I have quite determined to remain in the service. False hopes had long made me form other plans; but when I saw that I was mistaken, I altered my views, and fully determined not to be so weak again.

I am forgetting to tell you of the miseries of the journey. I was travelling with two captains near Frankfort-on-the-Oder, when we were stopped by some partisans, who were nothing but Prussian prisoners escaped into the woods. They robbed us of everything that we had: I could only save six *louis* and a *ducat* that I had sewn into my waistcoat. At Berlin I got an attack in the throat that nearly killed me. A kind doctor attended mo for twelve days, and would not take any money, saying that he was too glad to have made the acquaintance of a French officer. We are really much considered in this country, both on account of our-exploits and our want of pride. They compare us to their officers, who were empty and insolent. They do not gain by the comparison their pride is greatly abased: Berlin is quieter than in the time of the king, according to the statement of the inhabitants; provisions much cheaper, though there is less trade.

I do not in the least expect to join the legions that are in process of formation. Except the Imperial Guard, or the Royal Guard of Holland, which I do not like at all, there is not a corps for which I would exchange my own. According to appearances, I shall be captain in three years.

To his sister Phillis

Besançon, 1807: Though I have become somewhat of a philosopher, I have at this time some vexations that I endeavour in vain to stifle. The Government has just appointed a stranger to the regiment to the post of adjutant-major, to which I aspired. The Major is vexed at not having an officer of his own selection. This is a chance that will not occur again for a long time. The adjutant-major has not come yet; I am performing the duties, and showing a brave face to fortune.

I should be very glad to get on General Souhans' staff— it is very pleasant with a kind General. The place of captain attached that I might get is very nearly the same as that of aide-de-camp. He transacts all the business relating to the duties of the division, and a large portion of the General's correspondence. He is obliged to have two horses in war time; the pay is 180 francs a month, and forage, which is very nice.

Thus, wounded at Pultusk, and unable to follow his comrades in arms, he did not see the battle of Eylau, a contestable victory, the achievement of Murat's horsemen more than of Bonaparte's combinations, and a premonitory sign in the eyes of Benningsen, the Russian Commander-in-chief, of a startling retaliation; nor that of Friedland, 'the daughter of Marengo,' as said the Corsican hero in the imaginative language affected by the people of the South; nor the other various military events that led to the peace of Tilsit.

What an error of the conquering autocrat was the imperial Utopia destined to increase the Empire of the Czars with Bessarabia and Finland, to alienate Turkey and Sweden from France, and, lastly, to prepare in the regions of the North a centre of resistance to the desires of its author! The vanquished of Austerlitz and Friedland became, thanks to combinations, less worthy of Caesar than of Charles XII.; the heir-presumptive of Constantine was to bring about the fall of the 'great man,' whose friend he proclaimed himself before a gallery of kings. Anyway, the Treaty of Presburg was going to secure a moment's repose to Europe, exhausted and out of breath; while no one could then prophesy all its results.

CHAPTER 7

In Spain (1808–9)

Thomas Bugeaud had been for two years a lieutenant of Infantry of the Line (June 30, 1808) when he obtained leave for six months. This was the first time since his enlistment that he made so long a stay in Périgord. Home life, the affection he so much needed, his native air, inspired him afresh with disgust at military life—a disgust that he had so often displayed in his letters to his sister Phillis. So he decided, one fine day, to break with the past, and it was without hesitation or regret that he wrote to the Minister and sent in his resignation. His sister, Antoinette, offered to carry his letter herself to the post in the town. But, on consultation with her other sisters, she carefully locked up the important missive enclosed in a sheet of paper. The young man, delighted at having made up his mind, and proud of having regained his liberty forever, set himself seriously to the study of agriculture with the help of his sister Phillis. Nevertheless, he was beginning to be surprised at the Minister's delay in acknowledging the receipt of his resignation, when, instead of the final release that he expected, it was an order to join his regiment that he received. All was explained; his sisters' plot was discovered and forgiven; and the poor officer, who had so gladly renounced the glorious profession of arms, went to join his regiment, the 116th of the Line, which had just been sent to Spain.

The peace of Tilsit might have made Sub-lieutenant
Bugeaud believe for a moment that his desires would
be fulfilled. Isolated from all Europe by the checks to
her allies, and especially by the bad faith with which she
had repaid their assistance, England would be forced, in
the opinion of the politicians of the time, to behold, as
an envious but impotent observer, the elevation of the
Empires of the East and West, the two divisions of the
civilised world.

But the new pacificator of Europe had not despoiled
the conqueror of Italy and Austria in order to spend the
latter part of a career already so eventful in the administrative organization of his dominions. One day this indefatigable winner of crowns noticed Spain, and having at a
single glance comprehended its resources, and its strange
government, he determined to conquer it.

Soon afterwards Charles IV., the possible heir of the
crown of France, placed the States of the Emperor Charles
V. and Philip V. in the hands of Monsieur Bonaparte, Lieu-
tenant-General of the armies of Louis XVIII., who inter-
fered in the internal discords of the Peninsula in the name
of outraged morality.

The people displayed a less accommodating humour
than their King. Everything on which Bonaparte had
reckoned seemed to turn against him. The young Spaniards learnt in a new kind of catechism that Satan was in
three persons, Napoleon, Murat, and Godoy.

With the feverish activity peculiar to the people of the
South, who are condemned by the consequences of efforts
as excessive as they are momentary to ages of stagnation,
the Spaniards organized, in a few months, an insurrectionary government and a regular defence. The Juntas, equal in
number to the provinces, who at first had dearly paid the
penalty of local ideas, formed the central Cortes of Cadiz.
From this provisional capital, continually exposed to the
fire of the French batteries, were soon to issue the civil
and military liberators of Spain.

Upon this rock, surmounted with a fortress backed by the ocean, which constituted the whole European empire of the prisoner of Valençay, the sword of Napoleon was to be broken. At the moment of this explosion, Madrid was not forgetful that she was the head of Spain. The War of Independence commenced on the threshold of the royal palace. The second of May saw Castilian valour, forgotten the day before, blaze forth into light, and was the commencement of an era of glory.

For the first time did Lieutenant Bugeaud fight against a popular rising. What impression was produced on the future sword of the monarchy of July, by this war, without rule or law, but undertaken, it is true, in the name of the national religion, invaded country and dethroned king? The following letter, which does not appear to reflect the ferocity so long attributed by fable to 'the general of Transnonain,' will answer that question.

To his sister Antoinette

Madrid, 10th May, 1808: Your conscience is very tranquil, very approving, my dear Toiny; because I have not written to you ten times, you think you have nothing to blame yourself for. Well, you are wrong, you are very much to blame, not only for the harm you have done, but for the good you have neglected to do. Do you think that a poor soldier, away from any kind of pleasure, is not worth consideration, and ought you not to have relieved his weariness with several long letters? Remember that I read them at least six times the first day every two hours, and think of them meanwhile. I spend a happy day. Thus you are to blame. This is demonstrated, and so for the future be more wise.

You do not expect to hear the sound of guns and musketry; well, put cotton-wool in your ears, for you will be cannonaded. The populace of Madrid took a fancy to revolt on the second of May. They seized upon straggling

Frenchmen and cut their throats, then ran to the arsenal, took possession of it, dragged out guns, seized upon fire-locks, and began a little war in the streets with some French pickets. On our side we were not inactive. The assembly was beaten, we hurried to the city, and their success was but brief. We attacked them vigorously upon all points. They were overthrown, their guns taken, and in one hour this confused mass existed no longer. The same day a good many of the guilty were shot.

We lost some men in this action. I got out of it for a bruise and a slight scratch. The insurgents wished to mur-der our sick in the general hospital, but the strongest of these broke open the stores of arms and exterminated their assailants. Peace appears to be restored; but there is no de-pending on it, though the Prince is doing his utmost to quiet minds by his proclamations and his generosity to many of the guilty. He behaved with humanity, stopping our vengeance at several points at the moment when the carnage was most dreadful.

I assure you I am not much at ease when walking through the streets; I always have my hand on my sword, for there were daily assassinations before the revolt, and these gen-tlemen look our moderation for weakness. Now they are more gentle. Do you think that this little life is better than the gun and game-bag that you tell me of?

I assure you it is not a good time for playing the flute at night under a beauty's windows, and besides we have no leisure. So the article of love goes but badly in general. livery one complains of a dearth of intrigues, and perhaps I am one of the most lucky, though that is not much. A pretty little French milliner promised to love me for three days, and to go on after that if I am alive. She says, by way of reason, that our loves being birds of passage one cannot promise for long. My answer was that, the proofs must not be migratory, and begged for some on the spot that they might be permanent. The answer was that if I got, them, perhaps in three days I should not ask for a continuance, and must wait. I yielded to these grand reasons, but asked for pledges; and was given a ring and lent the *Lettres à Emilie*. I begged her to read them with me in order to furnish me with applications. You have the whole account of my Spanish loves, for you know that we have them in every country. You do not tell me about the truffles, nor my dog Polisson.

This explosion of patriotism, extraordinarily exaggerated in importance by the fertile imagination of the Spaniards, was in reality the commencement of the war, most sacred, most embittered, and most glorious to the people who maintained it, mentioned in contemporary European history.

Less than a year after the revolt of Madrid, Lieutenant Bugeaud was engaged in the capture of Saragossa. What man awake to the name of patriotism knows not the legend, if not the history, of this epic defence? In every age a town of Iberia has been a self-devoted holocaust for the national glory. Saragossa was a match for Saguntum and Numantia. And so the French were imbued with admiration for this improvised army, these public or private edifices transformed into fortresses, these heroic leaders torn from the charms of indolence, like Palafox, or the peace of a monastery, like Merino. The young officer's letter bears the impress of sadness; and shows the reader all the admiration he felt for this people with whom he was compelled to fight.

To his sister Phillis

Bivouac before Saragossa, Feb. 12, 1809: I have received, my dear Phillis, your little letter full of great reproaches, and, as I do not deserve them, I will not make excuses. I wish to direct your anger and mine against the Spanish assassins, who murder a great many couriers, though all precautions are taken. So complaints about correspondence are universal. The colonel of the regiment has received your letter of inquiry about me; he tells me he will answer it, but, for fear he should forget to reassure you, I do not miss the chance of an officer who is going to France as escort to a wounded general. I can write freely to you, for he will post the letter after passing Bayonne, and so there will be no fear of its being opened.

We are still before this cursed, this infernal, Saragossa. Although we took their ramparts by storm more than a fortnight ago, and are masters of part of the town, the inhabitants, stirred up by the hatred they bear us, by the priests and fanaticism, seem to wish to bury themselves under the ruins of their city, after the pattern of old Numantia. They defend themselves with incredible determination, and make us buy the smallest victory very dear.

Every convent, every house, holds out like a citadel, and every one has to be besieged by itself. The whole is disputed foot by foot, from the cellar to the loft, and it is not until everyone is killed with bayonet thrusts or thrown out of window that we call ourselves masters of a house. As soon as we have conquered one, there come upon us from the next house, through holes made for the purpose, grenades, shells, and a rain of musketry. It is necessary to raise barricades and cover ourselves very speedily, till measures are taken for attacking this fresh fort, and that can only be done by piercing the walls, for traversing the streets is impossible; the whole army would perish in them in a couple of hours.

It was not enough to make war in the houses, it is carried on beneath the earth. An art no doubt invented by devils leads the miners beneath the building held by the enemy. A large quantity of powder is laid there, fired at a given signal, and the wretches fly into the air or are buried beneath the ruins. The explosion makes the enemy evacuate the neighbouring houses in fear of the same fate. We are posted very near, and rush into them as quick as we can. This is how we make our way in this wretched city.

You may imagine how many men such a war must cost. How many young fellows, the hope of their families, have already perished among this rubbish! Our brigade has already lost two generals. General Lacoste, of the Engineers, a young man of the greatest promise who was not long from school, but already made one of the Emperor's aides-de-camp, has fallen a victim to his devotion, as well as so many others. There is not a day when there are not some officers among the dead—many more than in proportion to the soldiers, because the enemy, firing with certain aim when we make the attack, select their victims.

Oh, my dear, what a life, what an existence! It is now two months that we have been between life and death, corpses and ruins. If we get all the advantage from this war that is expected, it will be bought very dear. But the most fearful thing is to think that our labours and our blood may not be of use to our country. I always remember these lines of Voltaire—

Encore si pour votre patrie
Vous saviez vous sacrifier;
Mais non, vous vendez votre vie
*A ceux qui veulent la payer.**

Who can foresee the end of so many ills? Happy they who may catch a glimpse of it.

I write very sadly to you, my dear; but what would you have? One's mind is affected. No doubt if I had hopes of

---

* If only you knew how to sacrifice self for your country; but no, you sell your life to any that will buy it.

seeing you again soon I should be more cheerful; but, alas, that moment is far removed. While wailing its coming, may God preserve your health and happiness, and He will grant my most cherished desires.

Saragossa was at last conquered, and Palafox went to swell the number of his countrymen detained in France until the terrible reckoning of 1814. This siege, almost as much renowned to the north as to the south of the Pyrenees, was worth captain's rank to Lieutenant Bugeaud. And yet at this time the future Duke d'Isly seemed less concerned about his promotion than about that Périgord which he so ardently desired to revisit in order to resume his former habits there.

To his sister Phillis

Pampeluna, 20 March, 1809: How can I contrive, my dear Phillis, to express to you my joy and my sorrow? These two feelings present such a contrast, that it is hard to believe they can exist in one head at the same moment. However, that is what has happened to me to-day, but it is true that my sorrow is greater than my joy. To talk of the bad first.

You know I was in hopes that my return to France, or a journey into Germany, would procure me the great pleasure of being a witness of the first day of your happiness. In addition to this pleasant anticipation, there was the expectation of a journey to Bordeaux, by the colonel's orders, to buy musical instruments for our regimental band. I had the order in my pocket, and was ready to go, when the order to turn back into Spain arrived; my captain was ill, and no officer with the company but one only eighteen years old. The colonel told me he could not send me away, for a grenadier company could not go on a campaign without an officer to command it. Imagine my annoyance at the information, but I could not say a word.

There was talk of another siege, it would have risked the loss of all I had won at the siege of Saragossa. So off I went, and here I am at Pampeluna, where we have this morning been reviewed by the governor. While we were under arms, the colonel also was preparing a surprise for me as I am doing for you now, called me, addressed me as captain and handed me my commission! This is the cause of my rejoicing.

Our general of division is dead; that is the fifth since our entrance into Spain, four by the enemy's fire, and one by the prevailing sickness.

To his sister Hélène

Saragossa, 30 April, 1809: Your kind letter found me at Saragossa, where I have been for several days. A false alarm made us leave our cantonments to concentrate near the capital. Now it seems that the enemy have not made offensive movements. We have lost a good deal by these changes; the soldiers do not get such good food, we have to take up new ways, and change our mode of life according to the places we are sent to. Certainly I do not think that it would be advantageous to get into the guard with my rank, and those who say so are much mistaken. A captain in the guard ranks with a *chef-de-bataillon* in the line, and he can only exchange as such, indeed there are several who have gone out as majors.

This is a very evident advantage. Now to consider the difficulty that there is to get the rank of *chef-de-bataillon* in the line. There are eight captains for each *chef-de-bataillon*, and so there are eight candidates. Now I am the youngest captain of my regiment, and so have no ground to hope to be chosen in preference to my comrades. Let us then try to gain at once a rank that I cannot win here for a long time.

I am very thankful for the remembrances of the C——.
Please inform them of my thanks for their kind wish to
be useful to me, and my great desire to be in a position to
know them better. I embrace you with my whole heart.

Fortune was already turning against the man she had loaded with favours. The resistance of Spain was preparing the
public mind for the fatal campaigns of Russia and Saxony.

After a short stay at Saragossa, the new-made captain
twice crossed the north-west of Spain in search of the un-
approachable enemy whom the Grand Army was never to
bring to submission. These marches and counter-marches,
that go to make up almost all wars of this kind, caused him
to be present at the combats of Moria and Balahite, and
gained him the epaulette of superior officer.

To his sister Phillis

Saragossa, 29 September, 1809: I did not choose to answer your last letter immediately, my dear Phillis, because
I waited to be able to tell you something positive as to
the commission you gave me about the Spaniard. At last I
determined to mention it to Combemoreau himself. I discharged it with exactitude to please you us well as our rela-
tion; but I did nothing for the Aragonese peasant. I detest
that class of assassins and fanatics too much. However, the
brother of Gregorio has showed me much gratitude for the
information I gave him.

We remain at Saragossa, to our weariness and the drain-
ing of our purses. Everything is so dear, that the pay of
lieutenants and sub-lieutenants is not enough for them to
live upon. This wretched city still feels the disastrous effects of the siege. It is depopulated, and the inhabitants that
are left are so mournful that they freeze everything around
them. No amusing society, no *tertullias* (evening parties). All
remain shut up in their houses.

I cannot tell you how weary I am of this town; I go so far as to wish to he campaigning to get away from this cursed place. The only resource we have against this weary time is to eat, drink, and sleep; and the only eatables here are brought us by Frenchmen, who, attracted to the army by interest alone, take advantage of the circumstances to devour our substance.

Our future does not appear likely to he brighter. If peace is not made in Austria, affairs here will go dragging. We are strong enough to beat the enemy, but not to pursue him after the, victory. This cursed Peninsula is so large and so mountainous, that it would take three hundred thousand men to hold it in such a way as to ensure its speedy subjection. What we have done till now is of hardly any use. We have occupied several provinces which have risen again as soon as we left them; and even those we hold today are filled with little parties who, too weak to attack the army, fall upon small detachments, badly escorted convoys, couriers, orderlies, &c.

But this is melancholy talk enough; I must repair the effect it has had by telling you that nothing is wanting to my satisfaction but a better political condition. I am in a regiment that I look upon as a second home; my comrades like me; I think my chiefs value me, for they give me daily proofs of it; I command a fine company, well clothed, well disciplined, that cannot, fail to get me credit when there is an action. What is wanting to my happiness? Could I reasonably hope for such a good result when I entered the service without interest, without those brilliant talents that enable a young man always to make his way if he knows how to use them?

By the way, it is as well to let you know that I expect to remain a long time in the new rank I have just gained. It is not uncommon to see captains who have been so for fifteen years. There are in a regiment twenty-eight captains; there are so many competitors for one place of *chef-de-bataillon* that may chance to be vacant; I tell you all this that you may not be impatient in a few years' time. If I am a superior officer by the time I am thirty-two, I shall be well pleased.

I am very anxious to know if my business with Patrice is settled. Do you know I have written to him twice, now several months ago, and he has not answered?

Tell me what has become of Dubois in the turmoil. If you could give him a useful present, you would do me a favour.

If you know any young men who wish, or who ought, to enter the service, well brought up, and able to write a good hand, you may, in my name, boldly advise them to go before the Prefect and engage for the 116th regiment: the depot is at Aire, in Gascony. I promise them that, if they have the qualifications named above, they will be sergeants within six months. If you are interested in some of those who embrace this career you must inform me of their arrival at the depot. I will ask to have them sent to the battalions in the front, and then I will give them a good pat on the shoulder till they get the rank of sub-officer, and then it only depends on themselves to get made officers.

I go after game here whenever I have time. I kill a great many fat quails, very often I have wished you could have a dozen of them.

Just as I am writing come two bits of news: one—neither good nor had—is our departure from Saragossa on an expedition; the second is this, very bad for the regiment. There were coming to us from the depot two hundred pairs of shoes, four hundred sets of clothing, cloth for all the officers, epaulettes, thirty soldiers and twenty-nine musicians with their instruments. The insurgents in the mountains have attacked and taken this convoy, and that is a loss to us of 40,000 francs. That of our band, especially, will not be made good for a long time.

To his sister Antoinette

Barbastro, a town of the north of Aragon, not far from the Pyrenees, 1809: I received your kind letter, my dear Toiny, just at the moment when I had reached Saragossa, and found myself in front of the enemy; it made me for a moment forget that the cannon roared; and when we got the order to attack, the only painful feeling I experienced was that I could not read it a second time. So after the affair I fully recompensed myself. I read all you told me quite quietly; how delightful to hear what goes on in the country! But, here I have written a page, and told you nothing yet.

To begin, you know, perhaps, that after our return to Bayonne, in Spain, we were sent to Burgos, in the kingdom of Leon; that afterwards we made our expedition into Galicia, and went nearly to Corunna. Now take the map and follow me.

Here I am on the march to return to Leon, crossing the mountains and country of Vierys. Reaching the capital of the kingdom of Leon we find a gathering of troops, who are going on an expedition into the Asturias, and informed that we are to join them. We start by the steep cut road that leads to Oviedo, and the day before we ought to arrive at that capital, our brigade receives an order to turn back and go into Aragon, where the horizon was beginning to darken. We set off by long marches to return to the scene of our former glory. We rapidly cross Leon, Old Castile, the south of Navarre, and at last reach the plain of Saragossa.

What was our surprise to see all the baggage of the army in retreat, and all arrangements made to abandon a town that a few months before had cost so much trouble! We learnt that General Blake, having heard that the 5th corps had quitted Aragon, and that there were not more than 10,000 of the 3rd, had united 30,000 men of the armies of Valencia and Catalonia to seize upon our conquests, and was not more than two leagues from the capital.

The little French army was making a good show in presence of the enemy who were posted in the village of Maria, which is in a valley fringed by rather high mountains, and this favoured our small force. However, General Suchet had every reason to fear that he would be crushed by numbers, and for two days had been avoiding a general engagement in order to await our arrival. It was the 17th of June, at noon, that we effected our junction. It was announced to the army in order to give them confidence, and we immediately took our places in the line after having marched seven leagues; it was then I received your letter. The enemy, impatient to reach Saragossa, attacked us; as soon as he moved we went at him and in a moment the whole line was engaged. General Suchet made several very able manoeuvres, and the last decided the contest. While all the cavalry having gained the left flank of the enemy charged between his two lines, the whole of the infantry attacked in front with the bayonet. The boastful bands could not resist our impetuosity. They broke on all sides, and in less than half-an-hour we had gained a complete victory. The enemy left in our hands twenty-seven guns, three colours, a quantity of baggage, ammunition, a great number of killed, wounded, and prisoners. Among the last were two generals and several superior officers.

In this battle I became by chance captain of a light company. I had been sent with my company of the centre, under the orders of a captain of the light company of the same regiment who was senior to me; we were skirmishing in the olive groves and in a village on the bank of a little stream called the Warba; a post of consequence to keep. The poor captain of the light company was killed by a discharge of grape, and so I found myself commanding. The enemy tried several times to carry the post, but we always received them with such a sharp fire that they were obliged to drop their intention after leaving a number of dead before our shelters, from which we fired point-blank. By this means we prevented the enemy from passing by the only practicable road to turn the left of our army. It is true we were supported by a squadron, but they had no occasion to charge.

Alter the battle General Suchet came to the regiment, and asked who were the captains commanding the skirmishers in the village. I was put forward, he said, 'He must be saluted as captain of the Voltigeurs, for he looks to me like a skirmisher.' It is right to tell you that, I had a double-barrelled gun in a sling at my back, and this, added to the rest of my equipment, gave me a very swaggering look. I gave my thanks, and here I am commanding the green epaulettes and bugles. This does not suit my stature very well; but it is true that I am not cut off from the Grenadier company, and that is worth more, at least in respect of promotion.

After Moria came the combat of Balahite, where we took from the enemy all the guns he had left, and a number of prisoners. After this we crossed Aragon by forced marches, and here we are at Barbastro resting a little.

I cannot write any more to you as I have to take advantage of an opportunity of sending to Saragossa, and that does not happen every day. I beg you will tell Phillis about me, and Patrice and all the family, and you may, if desired, send my letter round.

Saragossa, September 2, 1809: I do not like to lose a moment in telling you anything that happens to me, good or bad, because you take the same interest in it as I do; it would, indeed, be treason against friendship not to toll you everything.

Well, you must know that I have been made captain of Grenadiers, that I command the first company, composed of a hundred and twenty of the finest men in the regiment and best behaved. Thus I hold an honourable position that I had no right to expect with my short amount of service. Another thing that should also go into the account is, that it is worth 600 francs more a year. So here I am, a little lord with an income of 2,400 francs. You can well understand that with this I am no longer obliged to live upon my little fortune, so you must be less careful in dealing with it.

I have nothing now to tell you; we are inactive, though surrounded with enemies, timid ones it is true, on account of their numerous defeats. It may be supposed that we shall make some attempt towards the end of this month, when the heat will be less.

I have mentioned Barbastro to you in another letter, we left it in the following way; a *chef-de-bataillon*, posted fourteen leagues from Saragossa, was attacked before day by a handful of insurgents; terror got the better of him, and he fled with all of his battalion he could collect, leaving two or three companies at the mercy of the supposed enemy. Not content with this cowardice, he immediately wrote a report to the General-in-Chief that he had been pursued by a considerable force, had lost a part of his battalion, and only got in after a terrible contest.

What happened? Why, the said companies, braver than their chief, chose to await a serious attack before retiring;

day came, they saw the weakness of the assailants, issued from the village, and saved the position. But the General, before he knew this, sent out his orders to all the troops to concentrate with all speed upon the capital. This is why I have left the agreeable Barbastro.

It is supposed that the *chef-de-bataillon* will be cashiered.

After the combat of Balahite, Commandant Bugeaud constantly followed the fortunes of Marshal Suchet. And so a few months after these engagements we find him in Catalonia engaged in the war of sieges that took place in that province.

CHAPTER 8

Lérida (1810-14)

Again we will leave the actor in the siege of Lérida himself to relate how this strong fortress lost its old reputation of impregnability.

To his sister Antoinette

Lérida, 4 June, 1810: I have written to you, my dear Toiny, by my Colonel, who is gone to France, but as that letter may be delayed a long time before it reaches you, and I do not like you to feel as if you might complain of me, I am going to address another to you. I hope you will cease to think that I make a favourite of Phillis, especially when you recollect she wrote oftener to me than you did, and it was but fair that I should answer her. Difference in affection has nothing to do with it, and I think I love you all equally—that is, all very much.

You leave politics and war to Phillis: you only want historical descriptions. Nevertheless, should not you be very glad to have an account of the siege and assault of Lérida? And after that I will tell you of the effect that our vigorous attack has produced upon the beauties as well as the plain ones.

The trenches were opened very near the works, with the audacity that is characteristic of the French Army. The works were continued with ardour when it was known that an army was coming to relieve the enemy. Nothing was suspended on that account; only the cavalry and some few battalions were detached to meet 12,000 of the best Spanish troops. The combat took place within sight of the city, and a diversion was attempted by a sortie of 2,000 men. Victory speedily declared itself in our favour. It was a brilliant charge of the 13th Cuirassiers and 4th Hussars that decided this affair, an everlasting triumph for our cavalry. The enemy's ranks were fearfully crushed, his infantry, put to the sword and broken, were obliged to lay down their arms, and not one man of the first division—7000 combatants—managed to escape. The cavalry only owed their safety to a speedy retreat. The garrison was not much more fortunate; they were driven back to the gates with the bayonet behind them.

In a few days batteries were established, and fired on the works, without much luck. The fire of the Castle crushed them, and in three hours they were silenced, and others had to be constructed. The bad weather was against us. However, five days afterwards forty guns were in position, and opened two large breaches.

The enemy must have expected the assault on that day; they were deceived by attacks made upon some formidable redoubts they held on another side, that were very bravely taken. Next day the assault of the place was ordered, ten picked companies, mine being one of them, were in orders, and assembled in the trenches nearest to the breaches.

About six in the evening, at the signal of four cannon-shots, we dashed on like lightning. The walls were escaladed, the works were entered, several barricades were broken, and our enemies perished in crowds under our blows. A gate leading to the quays delayed us a moment: then several of our brave men were killed by a point-blank discharge. At last the gate was broken; we entered in a mass, racing with one another. Every man wanted to be first to strike, nothing could stop us—bayonets, shot, and pikes could not daunt our ardour. I have the luck of penetrating the mass with my company; I am the first to reach a fortified post, and I cut off a lot of the enemy whom we treated to the edge of the sword and the bayonet. The redoubts, the guns, the city, all fell into our hands. The terrified Spaniards took refuge in the citadel and carried alarm with them. A number of the inhabitants also took refuge there. The soldiers, greedy for pillage, scatter themselves about among the houses; carnage ceases, and gives place to scenes of quite another kind; the conquerors are everywhere seen in the arms of the vanquished—Carmelites, grey sisters, old women, young nuns, all experienced the transports of our Grenadiers, and several of them are said to have cried out, 'Oh, if we had known that this would be all we should not have been so much afraid.'

The day after this terrible one, the forts were terrified into offering to capitulate, and so in a short time we made ourselves masters of a formidable city that had seen the great Condé fail at the foot of its walls, and that the Duke of Orleans only took in 1707 after thirty-three days of open trenches. But the greatest advantage of our victory is that it has turned the minds of all the women in our favour. They were breathing nothing but revenge and detestation; today they have become so kind and gentle that there is no more need for an assault. By way of formality they exact the honours of war, and these are always granted them. We stay some days at Lérida; and already there is a talk of sieges of Valencia and Tortosa. Always beginning again!

Time passes, King Joseph has already lost and then regained his capital, where he only displays his power by acts of clemency, using in vain the most noble attribute which the constitutions of the age leave in possession of the rulers of the State. In the various provinces of the Peninsula the work of conquest only eventuated in barren victories.

Catalonia is divided into departments, organized upon the model of those of France; but the strong towns, the mountains, the isolated villages, everything that is guarded from our arms by art, nature, or solitude, still resist the invaders, and shelter the soldiers of independence. The heroic and patient adversaries of the Moors, waked up by the sound of the guns of Saragossa, and encouraged by daily partial successes, sustain the military ardour that enables them to hope for a final victory.

To his sister Phillis

At the bivouac of Tivisa (Catalonia), eight leagues from Tortosa, on the left bank of the Ebro, July, 1810: I am sorry to hear nothing of you, my dear Phillis, but I do not blame you. There are so many couriers intercepted I am very much afraid that either my letters have not reached you, or that your replies have fallen into the hands of some Spanish partisan, who probably has made very little account of what is so very dear to me. If these gentlemen would wish to be reconciled to me, let them send me your correspondence. I would content myself with making them prisoners; but, as they have not been gallant enough to do it, I declare war to the death against them, and, as often as any of them fall into my hands, I will send them to Pluto to teach them how to live.

I told you in my former letters that you might dispose of my little revenue as you pleased without being obliged to consult me.

I have given you an account of the siege of Lérida, and that I had gained some credit there. If I had possessed the least interest I should have been made a lieutenant-colonel. My colonel asked for this promotion for me, and Pascal told me he saw the application in the report that the general of division sent to Count Suchet. I do not know if it reached the Government. But I am not without some hopes, and two consecutive fights we have just had at Tivisa have refreshed them. The 116th Regiment has gained much credit. I will tell you this in place. I am going to begin by making you perfect in our earliest operations.

The Third Corps marched on the two sides of the Ebro towards Tortosa, to besiege it. This movement seemed to be in combination with Marshal MacDonald, who commands in Catalonia; but it seems that the shattered condition of his army, and the deficiency of magazines in this wasted country, prevented him from starting as soon as we did. Notwithstanding this difficulty, General Suchet established his headquarters at Nora, formed the blockade of the bridge-head of Tortosa, which is upon the right bank, and pushed up our division on the left bank to within two leagues of the place. He established two flying bridges for communication, the one at Tibinys, the other before Mora. Care was taken to protect them by field-works.

However, the Spanish army, not being attacked on the side of Taragona, turned all its attention to us. General Odonilla issued a proclamation, in which he exhorted all the inhabitants to join the army in order to throw us into the Ebro. He named for points of concentration Falcet and Tivisa, from which it was easy for him to hinder our communications, as well as the navigation of the Ebro. In fact, three thousand Spaniards and some hundreds of peasants came to occupy Tivisa. A similar number proceeded to the other point, at only four leagues distance.

General Suchet, informed of this, ordered the 115th and 116th on detachment to attack the men at Tivisa. The combat was not bloody; the enemy gave ground as soon as we met, leaving in our power a very few prisoners and some stores.

We remained holding this place to the number of seven hundred; the 115th returned to Mora.

On the sixteenth of July we were attacked by six thousand men, commanded by three generals. Our forces being dispersed over various hillocks that it was important to guard, it was not difficult to drive us from them. However, we only yielded foot by foot, and when being attacked by very superior forces we had reason to fear that we should be surrounded.

We made several brilliant charges, but at last were obliged to yield to numbers. We were successively deprived of all our positions, and found ourselves forced to retire by the road to Mora. I was entrusted with the duty of covering the retreat, during which I lost nineteen men; but having stopped the enemy in several places, I prevented them from taking advantage of the disorder that reigned in the column, as they could not have failed to make a great many prisoners.

General Abbé re-formed the column on a plateau covered with vines, and bounded by rather difficult ravines. The enemy manoeuvred in three columns; two tried to turn our flanks, and the third attacked us in front. A little audacity, with the help of a simple trick of war enough, got us out of the scrape. We had just received three fresh companies; two were placed at the head with mine, the third extended on the flanks to drive off the skirmishers. In this order we resolved to charge the centre column with the bayonet, judging, with reason, that the ravines would prevent the others from taking part in the action for some time.

We had been fighting all day in white linen *chakos*; we took them off and having done this rushed upon the column with the greatest vivacity. Astonished at our audacity, and supposing by the change of ornament that we had received a considerable reinforcement, they only fired once, and were thrown into horrible disorder. Without giving them time to rally, we pursued them with the bayonet at their flanks to the foot of a high hill, where they broke, leaving in our power their wounded and a great many prisoners. The rest, terrified at the defeat of the centre, escaped into the mountains. We pursued them till night, killing and wounding a large number of them.

This combat is a very evident proof that it is not numbers that decide the victory. A body inferior in number to its enemy, but composed of brave men, and directed by a man of skill, should fear nothing. It may encounter a momentary check, but its constancy and determination will furnish its chief with the means of seizing a fortunate opportunity, and repairing everything in a moment.

This little victory only served to prove our superiority; for, with a thousand men, we beat six thousand; but the results were not considerable enough to make the enemy abandon their projects. They were reinforced at Falcet; we at Tivisa. In a few days there will be a battle. The victory is not doubtful, they will be beaten; but I do not expect the action will be decisive, because the difficulties of the ground do not permit the action of our cavalry, and present a thousand ways of escape to a beaten army.

We lost in the affair of the 16th a *chef-de-bataillon* (we had one in succession who replaced him), three lieutenants and sub-lieutenants, twenty-two soldiers and sergeants, and forty-eight wounded. A very slight loss for so serious a conflict, with several bayonet encounters.

I think I shall be able to tell you that I am a member of the Legion of Honour. There are fourteen crosses for my regiment. The list is made, and I am at the top. It has been forwarded to the *Chancellerie*, and we expect our patents every day. As to the lieutenant-colonelcy, that is not so certain. However, as I have already told you, there is still hope. After the affair of the 16th, General Abbé said to me, 'Young man, I think I may promise you that you will be *chef-de-bataillon* before the end of the year.'

I tell you rather shamelessly of these flattering words addressed to a young man who follows the profession of arms, but, I hope it will not go beyond the family, and that you will judge me well enough to think that it is my great confidence in you that makes me thus communicative.

Write to me twice for once, and tell me the same things over again, for the roads have never been less scenic. As we advance in our conquests, the brigands multiply in our rear. There must be no army for us to go to work with them.

> Who could then foresee that the year 1812 which had just commenced, would see the Grand Army disappear among the snows of Russia, while in Spain every day brought on the capture of a fortress or the destruction of a guerilla? However, this desperate warfare was not nearly concluded.
>
> Marshal Suchet, the most notable organizer of the conquest of the Peninsula, made himself master of the city of Valencia and received the title of Duke.

To his sister Antoinette

Camp before Valentia, 1 January, 1812: We crossed the Guadalaviar on the 26th, and after a rather sharp encounter the city was very closely invested. General Blake, president of the insurrectionary *Junta*, is inside with 15,000 men. The rest of his troops have escaped to Alicante. Our army is superb, full of confidence, and rejoicing in an excellent spirit; that of the Spaniards, on the contrary, is entirely discouraged by its numerous defeats, and will soon be in want of everything. This difference of situation must very soon cause the fall of Valencia, and the conquest of the kingdom of that name. We opened the trenches last night, all is going on most excellently.

Among the letters of Thomas Bugeaud to his family we have found one dated from Barcelona, and addressed to an old servant of the family of La Piconnerie. We publish it, and think there is no need to call attention to its affecting simplicity and the exquisite sentiments it contains.

To M. Pierre Lionnet

Barcelona, 3 September, 1812: I was glad to receive your letter of congratulation; I even ought to say I was flattered by a good and old servant like you having preserved the remembrance of a man whom he only knew as a little child: it is more than a remembrance, it is interest and affection. I assure you I am very sensible of it. I have often thought of our estimable Lionnet, and always considered that be must be happy, for I knew that he possessed the qualities that must attract the friendship of the masters whom he served. I do not know why he left the family of Lajudie, but I presume that it was not his fault, and that another situation must have made up for his loss. If I was mistaken, my dear Lionnet, address yourself to Mdlle. Phillis, she has some funds of mine, and will send you some help. You need only present my letter to her, use it without formality or scruple.

It is true, my dear Lionnet, that I have prospered in the profession of arms; it has cost me more pain and self-devotion than it does others. I was without interest and without the brilliant education that promises great success; I have gained my rank by much toil, danger, and privation. I am well in health, and feel myself strong enough to make fifteen campaigns if they were wanted for the safety of our country, which cannot be.

Our affairs in Spain have been rather a failure, but I hope that we shall restore them in the coming campaign.

Adieu, my dear Lionnet, keep well, and believe in my attachment to you.

Granollen, 1813: I have delayed writing because I wished to tell you something definite as to my position. Fortune is very capricious towards me, she serves me in action, everywhere else she deserts me.

You know I had a well-founded expectation of being appointed colonel. Well, the minister sent me a major's commission for the army of reserve at Montpellier. Marshal Suchet was very much annoyed at it. He spoke to me with the greatest kindness, and changed my destination, giving me the command of the 14th of the line, and wrote again to the minister to press for my appointment as colonel to this regiment or to some other. This is my position. Henceforth please address me Major commanding the 14th of the line, 1st division of the army of Aragon and Catalonia.

I am going to join my regiment which is at Girona.

On the 10th I was attacked at Saint Vincent by nine battalions eighteen hundred horses, and four guns. It was not a fair match we had to halt, after delaying the enemy long enough to allow the troops from Barcelona to reach the fortified position of Esplugas. By the help of some small entrenchments, I maintained myself two hours upon the right bank, and killed and wounded three hundred men of the enemy. My loss was seventy wounded and seven killed.

A horse which my servant was bringing me was killed. I cared for him very much. It was an Andalusian that I had owned for three years.

The Marshal gave me a lot of praise for my defence of Bobregal. That is worth more than nothing. The enemy's project was to capture the garrisons of Saint Vincent and Molinos del Rey. Having missed their point they retired, and we resumed our positions, and kept them till the 19th. I learn that the advanced posts are pushed near Barcelona.

I think I told you that the convoy of money, that had my 7,000 francs, was robbed near Toulouse of a box with 10,000 francs. We are bringing an action against the carriers, but am afraid we shall lose, my loss will be 1,800 francs. Our pay is five months in arrears. I begin to be short of money. I think Marshal Soult's army is doing well, and there is no fear that the English will penetrate further.

An important personage has crossed Catalonia, who, they say, goes to propose peace to the Cortes. I look upon this negotiation as very difficult.

To his sister Phillis

Saint Vincent, near Barcelona, 22 December, 1813. Perhaps you will see in the Gazette that on the 10th of this month I captured a picket of thirty-five horse and an officer. I received flattering compliments from the Marshal. That is all I have got for three years. His desire to keep me in his *corps d'armée* has done me much injury. I should be colonel today if I had been major a year, and as I might have been, and his Excellency did not choose, under the excuse that he kept a regiment of his army for me.

A little Spanish servant has robbed me of nearly 800 pieces of Spanish gold; in return I have made booty of two fine horses worth 80 *louis*, that only cost me a little money, that I have made into a fund for the soldiers who were on the expedition. Each of them had 66 francs. Their cavalry is very well mounted.

A letter from Mont Marsan tells me of a victory gained over the Anglo-Spaniards before Bayonne. Marshal Soult's manoeuvres, if they are as said, were fine, wise, and bold.

Ah, my dear Phillis, when shall we meet? When shall we ccasc to disturb the world? Ah, without patriotism, how weary I should be of the first, of all professions! You will find me aged, I am beginning to turn grey; do not tell that to the fair ones of the country, they would take advantage of it, and I hope with a little attention to my toilette I may partly conceal the ravages of time.

Although the Duke of Albufera had managed to establish an appearance of organization in the kingdom of Valencia, whence King Joseph sometimes received assistance, none the less was it necessary daily to fight the little armed bands that intercepted all our communications and were supported by the English. The Spanish insurrection was at last to gain its point. But before leaving this country, to which he was attached by five years of struggle and fatigue, the late *vélite* of Austerlitz reproduces his first victories and gains the epaulette of Major (lieutenant-colonel).*

To his sister Antoinette

You do not write to me any more. Do you think that I do not care to get letters from you? You are quite mistaken. I love you, and consequently love to hear from you. I allow I write little; but you write still less, though you could do so more easily than I can. Every day I have five or six letters to write, without counting a good deal of other pen work. I

---

* In the Memoirs of Marshal Súchet, there is often mention of *Chef-de-Bataillon* Bugeaud, who gave proof on several occasions 'of capacity and intrepidity;' notably at the combat of Ordal. It is interesting to give an extract: *A section of Sappers marching with an advanced guard were among the first to reach the redoubt with the Voltigeurs. The enemy made an obstinate resistance, and twice drove us off. A second redoubt, placed very high and very near, crushed the assailants with its fire when they had made their way in. General Mesclop with his sword drawn brought them back with beat of drum; Chef-de-Bataillon Fenchères was wounded, and several brave men perished in the shock. At last the redoubt remained in our possession; almost all its defenders were killed. Immediately, Marshal Suchet advanced Habert's division to the left upon the road, and General Harispe's reserve followed Mesclop's brigade. The battalion of the 116th, led by Commandant Bugeaud, made a movement to turn the second redoubts by the left; they were at the same time attacked in front, as well as the retrenchments that supported their flanks on the crest of the hill. All were carried with a rush, and the enemy retreated, leaving many dead and wounded, covered by his cavalry.*

have besides, important business, and it will be much worse when I am colonel. Then you will owe me three letters for one. Do you quite understand?

Some time ago there was some news of me in the Gazette. It is possible that you may again see in it that I captured an English picket of thirty-five horse and an officer. They might say 'God damn' as much as they liked, but they had to capitulate.*

I am well in health, but a little sick at heart, yet I am not in love.

There is a singular fate against, my promotion. I often have a chance of attracting observation; my chiefs all say that, they wish me success, and I get nothing! Patience and the armour of patriotism.

<u>To his sister Phillis</u>

Girone, 13 February, 1814. I wrote to tell you I was made major, and that his Excellency had given me the command of the Fourteenth to recompense me, if possible, for the minister's harshness. I have the certainty that his Excellency the Marshal has done all he could for me. A letter from the War-Minister proves it. He tells me he is desired to express to me the Emperor's satisfaction at my good conduct at Ordal and on every occasion. I preserve this letter among my archives.

I send you a letter of good General Harispe, though my doing so shows some vanity. It is indeed extremely flattering, but from a sister I fear no criticism, You will see that I

---

* On the 9th, Suchet pushed a small corps by Bejer, between the Ordal and Sitjes, and on the 10th surprised, at the Ostel of Ordal, an officer and thirty men of the Anglo-Sicilian cavalry. This disaster was the result of negligence. The detachment after patrolling to the front had dismounted without examining the buildings of the inn, and some French troopers who were concealed within immediately seized the horses and captured the whole party.

must be very unfortunate if I am not a colonel very soon.

I have a very fine regiment which I much wish to keep. I do not know the 9th Light. I am aware that it has a brilliant reputation, but it must have lost most of its old soldiers.

The third part of our army, half the cavalry and all the light artillery, have marched for Lyons. We are on *Ter*, and I think we shall soon be on the *Fluvia*. There has been no fighting since that on the 16th. The general orders relating to that affair mention me in a very flattering way. I will compel the minister to give me promotion.

Our pay is reduced by a fifth as long as there is an enemy upon the soil of France. We get no pay; I shall soon be obliged to ask for money. I am, and long shall be, a poor devil. There are no riches to be gained in the profession of arms when it is honestly and nobly practised. But for the high pay of the kingdom of Valencia, I should be without a *sou*. There must be love of glory, for we get nothing else and buy it very dear. Our condition is most deceptive, and yet one becomes most incredibly attached to it; so much so, that it is very painful to become a civilian again; even when our physical powers no longer allow us to serve, we always want to run after this phantom of honour and glory. It was thus that Gil Blas left his pretty country at Livia to return to the court where he had experienced all the tricks of fortune.

To his sister Phillis

Moxente, 29th April, 1814. I received your letter of the 1st of April yesterday. It is very good, for it is very long, and I bargain with you to continue in the same style. The couriers come in regularly every ten days.

It is true that Colonel Rouelle has been made a general, and it is also very true that I had the greatest hopes of succeeding him in the 116th regiment. They were based upon the positive promises of the Marshal Duke of Albufera, and the wish of all my chiefs and comrades that it should be so. Everyone looked upon me as a colonel, and the officers congratulated me on it; but often the things that seem most certain escape us at the moment we think we hold them.

Success in the profession of a soldier depends much on chance and luck. It is not enough to be a good player, a man must be likewise lucky. Until now I have had the happiness of finding several opportunities of bringing myself into notice. Just lately again, at the combat of Yecla, the Marshal Duke of Albufera told me, 'Monsieur Bugeaud, a month ago I asked for a regiment for you, and you have just established a fresh claim. I greatly hope that you will have the 116th, at least I will ask for it till I have got it.'

After that you see that I might hope. Well, my dear, yesterday we received a letter addressed to the administration of the 116th from M. Chevalier, major of the 11th, to inform us that he is appointed colonel of the 116th, General Rouelle is quite distressed at it.

So my promotion is stopped till there is another bit of luck. I have desired Hélène to give you a long letter in which I tell her all about our combats of the 10th 11th, 12th, and 13th of April.

One of our countrymen, M. Mesclop de Bergerac; has just been made General, he is a great friend of mine; I enclose two of his letters written to me after some small expeditions in which I was fortunate.

It was unlucky for me that they wanted to do too much for me. If an officer's cross had been asked for, it would have been got. A colonelcy was asked for—a much better thing, for it is the road to everything, and therefore I shall have nothing.

I think the Marshal is not on good terms with the War Minister, because at first he only addressed himself to the Major-General (Berthier). Now that the latter is ill, the Duke de Feltre does not care to be of service to the Marshal. Alas, it is on all these petty feelings that our promotion is dependent, when His Majesty is not with the army.

To his sister Phillis

Barcelona, 29th August, 1814: I am at Barcelona, my dear Phillis, as a bit of a change from the life in camps and mountains. This city is beautiful, and well worth a journey of several miles to see.

I hear that a courier is to start for France tomorrow, and will not lose this chance of telling you that I am well and always love you.

It is probable that we shall not be long before we come near to France. The force of circumstances draws us that way, but our immediate enemy does not drive us. The army of Aragon is still respected. Since we retreated we have not, fired a shot.

My heart is torn with all that I hear of the army in the north of Spain. It is very sad for us thus to lose the fruits of our splendid labours, &c, &c. I say no more. I suffer too much.

> The Emperor had an especial esteem for Marshal Suchet, and he considered him one of the best French generals. 'What he writes,' said Napoleon, 'is worth even more than what he says, and what he does is worth more than what he writes—-just the contrary to many others.'
>
> The commandant of the two armies of Aragon and Catalonia had noticed his officer Bugeaud. Between the young corporal of Austerlitz, the future Duke d'Isly, and the Marshal Duke of Albufera, there was thenceforward a kind of mysterious relationship of honour, kindliness, and

glory. Napoleon said that if he had possessed two marshals like Suchet in Spain, not only should he have conquered the Peninsula, but he should have kept it. That just, conciliatory, administrative mind, that soldierly tact and courage had gained for him incredible success. Napoleon added, 'It is vexatious that sovereigns cannot create men like that.'

The five campaigns made by Marshal Suchet in Spain as General-in-Chief will remain as an imperishable example of everything requisite in wise combinations, audacity, and dexterity for establishing the domination of a foreign army in the midst of a great people rising against them.

It was on the 1st of January, 1814, that the invasion of the allied armies commenced on all the boundaries of the empire, except on the side of the Alps, still covered by the Viceroy Prince Eugene Beauharnais at the head of the army of Italy. As soon as war was kindled in the heart of France, it was necessary to take into consideration the relinquishment of the occupation of Spain, and to evacuate the kingdom that the Treaty of Valençay restored to King Ferdinand.

On the 14th of January, by orders from the War Minister, the Duke de Feltre, ten thousand foot-soldiers, and two-thirds of the cavalry, quitted Barcelona. This first column was directed upon Lyons, to be followed speedily by the last remains of our army of occupation.

Commandant Bugeaud went with the last portions, and left Spain at the same time as the General-in-Chief. The instructions were to hold back the enemy before him, either to secure the safety of the garrisons or to protect the territory of France, and make his arrangements to do his part in covering the heart of the threatened empire.

In the certificates of service given to Colonel Bugeand, under the heading, 'Distinguished behaviour, wounds,' are found the following entries, given complete:

CAMPAIGNS IN SPAIN

At the storm of Lérida, 13th May, 1810, the breach was scaled with courage, but the assailants on reaching the quay were stopped by the active fire of six light guns and a number of muskets. Captain of Grenadiers Bugeaud, at the head of his company, rushed upon the guns and spiked them. On this occasion he himself killed several soldiers and gunners.

On the 15th of July, 1810, at the combat of Tivisa, Captain of Grenadiers Bugeaud was ordered to protect the retreat. He did so with the greatest coolness and courage, and was the first to resume the offensive, which decided the result of the combat.

At the siege of Tortosa the enemy made a general sortie on the 28th of December, 1810, Captain Bugeaud with his company cut off four to five hundred men, bayonetted a large number, took some, and chased the rest as far as the glacis. This action gained him honourable mention in general orders.

During the siege of Tarragona, May 11, 1811, Chef-de-Bataillon Bugeaud was sent with seven companies to relieve the garrisons of Amposta and La Rápita. Attacked by four battalions and three hundred horse at daybreak, he fell on the enemy's flank, beat them completely, rescued the. two garrisons, took five guns served by English gunners, a hundred and fifty men, and a colonel.

On the 1st November, arriving at Barrocca to reinforce General Mazzuchelli with six companies of the Fourth Italians, he caught sight of the band of Duran, composed of two thousand five hundred foot-soldiers, and three hundred horse, in pursuit of some companies of the First Italian Regiment, he attacked this enemy in flank, made them lose hold, drove them from several strong positions, and compelled them to retreat, leaving a large number of killed and wounded. On the 3rd he was detached to go to the relief of Alumnia, and on the 4th he was attacked by all the bands united, to the number of six thousand foot-soldiers and eight hundred horse. He was frequently surrounded during the retreat he made from Alumnia to Muela, but he always broke the enemy who attacked his line, repulsed several charges of cavalry, and reached Saragossa with two-thirds of his men, including his wounded, nearly all of whom he brought off.

On the 20th of November he was detached by General Musnier against the band of Campillo. On the 23rd, at midnight, he surprised the cavalry of that chief, killed twenty men, took thirty-two horses, twelve soldiers, and the commanding officer. He immediately marched against the infantry, hoping to surprise them, but could only reach them at daybreak; he fell upon them very speedily, killed several officers, about a hundred men, and dispersed the rest.

The 1st of September, 1812, he was detached with four companies and twenty-four horse to destroy a collection of guerrillas in the valley of Concenteyna. He attacked them at daybreak and dispersed them. As he returned, these brigands joined by a large number of peasants attacked his flanks. By a pretended flight he drew them into an open space, where he killed three hundred.

The 26th of December, 1812, he was ordered to surprise the garrison of Ibi, threecompanies and forty horse. One of his detachments alarmed the enemy too soon, nevertheless he took two hundred and sixteen men and fourteen horses, a captain and a lieutenant of the dragoons of Almanza.

At the combat of Ordal, Sept. 13, 1813, he determined the capture of the redoubts and the position by a vigorous attack on the right flank of the enemy, carried out with four companies of his battalion.

On the 13th December, 1813, an ambush that he placed near the pass of Ordal captured thirty-five English horse and an officer.

CAMPAIGN IN FRANCE

The 14th of June, 1815, he was in charge of the left attack upon the Piedmontese line. He seized upon Conflans (Savoy), beat the Chasseurs Robert and the Regiment of Piedmont; he made two hundred prisoners, and killed or wounded five or six hundred men. On the 23rd he captured a company at Moutiers. On the 28th he was attacked by seven thousand Piedmontese and Austrians under the orders of Marshal Trenck. He retook the town of l'Hôpital three times at the head of his Grenadiers, and threw a column of two thousand men who tried to turn his flank into the river. After seven hours' fighting he held possession of the place. In this affair he killed and wounded twelve hundred men, and made five hundred prisoners. His force was fifteen hundred men and forty horse.

CHAPTER 9

1814 and 1815

The first of January, in the year 1814, was a sad day for France. The armies of the coalition hedged our frontiers; on all sides the cities and territories were overrun; lastly, a bloody and obstinate strife was waged around the capital. During the short campaign in France, when all the resources of a wonderful mind were developed, hope did not abandon Napoleon I., until the last moment, when he saw that everything was slipping from him. Victory at last was weary of following him; the army was worn out and its strength exhausted; the marshals were glutted with plunder, their devotion exhausted.

On the evening of December 3, the Emperor left headquarters, and went to Paris to receive as formerly, in prosperous times, the great bodies of the State assembled at the Tuileries. A piteous and heart-rending comedy!

The sovereign's reply to the embarrassed compliments of the Senate was short and significant.

'Bearn, Alsace, Franche-Comté, and Brabant are invaded,' said he. 'The cries of these members of my family distract my soul. I summon the French to. the assistance of the French; I call the French, of Paris, Brittany, Normandy, Champagne, Burgundy, and the other departments, to the aid of their brethren. Will they leave us to misfortune? Peace and the deliverance of our territory should be our rallying word. The stranger will flee or sign peace on terms of his own proposing, at sight of all this people in arms. This is no time to speak of recovery of the conquests we have made.'

France made no response.

Two months later, the Senate, in obedience to circumstances, and following the will of the nation, as well as their own instinct, put the climax to the defection and registered it. On the 3rd of April, 1814, a proclamation from the Senate announced that 'Napoleon having forfeited the throne, hereditary right is abolished in his family, and the people and the army are released from the oath of fidelity.'

Two days afterwards the house of Bourbon was restored in France.

To resist the decrees of fate would have been madness. The people also, wearied and ruined, impatiently clamoured for peace. As for the army, it must be avowed that it gave the new government a cordial reception. Excepting a few generals and soldiers, who remained faithful, and who were attached to the Emperor by some special favour or personal bond, all received the accession of King Louis XVIII with acclamations and enthusiasm.

The army of Spain, with which was Major Thomas Bugeaud, had been neglected and sacrificed by their master more than any other corps. The letters written by the young officer during the six years he passed in Spain often express great discouragement, and very pardonable disgust. In spite of most brilliant deeds of arms, the reiterated recommendations of his immediate superiors, even those of the commander-in-chief of the army of Catalonia, Marshal Suchet, remained without result and unanswered.

It seems that this neglect arose from carelessness in the offices, and the ill-feeling of the War Minister, the Duke de Feltre, against Marshal Suchet, the Duke of Albufera.

Although Thomas Bugeaud had won his corporal's stripes on the field of Austerlitz, the son of the Marquis de la Piconnerie, enlisted at twenty years of age among the *vélites* of the guard, did not long remain subject to the spell of the great conquering Caesar. We have seen him several times during the campaign in Germany ardently longing with sighs to return to his country, and the long and curious correspondence he kept up with his sisters at this time frequently contains bitter criticisms on the profession of arms, which he had entered against his inclination.

When the royal family returned to France, the 14th regiment of the line, in which Thomas Bugeaud held the rank of Major, was ordered to garrison Orleans. In a short time came his appointment as Colonel. We give his letter informing his sister of this happy event. It is almost always to his elder sister Phillis, his faithful and devoted confidante, that the Marshal's long correspondence is addressed, beginning in 1804, on his enlistment in the *vélites* of the guard, and affectionately preserved in the family.

Nothing was concealed from his sister. He communicated to her his impressions, his secret thoughts, all the actions of his life. We know of nothing more touching than this tender and filial affection of the soldier towards her who stood in the place of mother to him, and by whose side were passed his earlier years in the old home of La Durantie. This deep feeling never failed. Madame de Puyssegenez throughout her life retained the ascendancy she had possessed over her brother during his infancy and youth.

To his sister Phillis

La Ferté-Saint-Aubin, near Orleans, 12 July, 1814: This very moment I am informed that the King has made me a colonel by a decree of June 11. So I was a colonel when I was at Puyssegenez. Fortune is wonderfully kind to me, and seems to reserve my pleasures so that I may be continually receiving one. So she did not choose me to know of my promotion while I was with you; it would have been too much good at once.

The favour I have just received is very great, considering the actual circumstances. Several old colonels were asking for the 14th. If I had not been appointed, I should have had to compete with fifty-seven majors my seniors. And most likely I should have been sent about my business with half pay.

I request you to inform the whole family in Périgord of my appointment, and ask you afterwards to send my letter to Hélène, who will tell Toiny; but no, I think, though very busy, I will write to Hélène, and you need only undertake Périgord.

I shall reach Orleans tomorrow, and shall enter it at the head of 1,100 men in fine order. Marshal Suchet, who saw us when he came to Vierzon, told me it was the finest and largest regiment in the whole army. Everything is going on as well as I could possibly desire. The only thing wanting to my complete satisfaction would be to keep the brave officers, who have contributed so much to my being appointed their colonel. I fear a good many of them will be lost.

I shall be able to write little for a fortnight. I shall have much to do for the new organization of my regiment.

The city of Orleans, ardently Royalist, was very eager to celebrate the return of the princes after their long exile. The newly promoted colonel enthusiastically joined in all these manifestations, and especially in the fetes given by the city on the occasion of a visit of the Duchesse d'Angoulême.

Thus passed at Orleans the first period of the Restoration, without incident, until the return from the island of Elba. It has been stated that in March, 1815, at the time of the Emperor Napoleon's landing at Cannes, Colonel Bugeaud, having proclaimed that he was going to fight the usurper, himself gave his soldiers the signal to desert the royal cause.. According to an account then current, Colonel Bugeaud did not even wait to leave Orleans before declaring himself, but made his soldiers mount the tricoloured cockade in the suburb Bourgogne.

We believe these statements are unfounded. First, it is established by official documents that the scene supposed to have taken place in the Faubourg Bourgogne is imaginary. Some mischievous speeches having passed among the soldiers of his regiment, Colonel Bugeaud immediately checked them. Marshal Moncey, first inspector-general of gendarmerie, had informed the Minister-at-War of the reports current on this matter.

There was no imputation then cast upon the conduct of Colonel Bugeaud, and yet he had left Orleans several days before. He had already reached Montargis, where he was to operate with the army corps intended to oppose Napoleon if he should advance from Burgundy. The Minister-at-War, the Duke de Feltre, wrote on the 16th of March, 1815, to Colonel Bugeaud, concerning the bad spirit some of his soldiers had exhibited at Montargis.

I know, it is true, that, full of zeal, and a sense of your obligations, you, as well the officers, have done all you could to restrain the men, and keep them to their duty. But these measures are not sufficient.

Now, these very acts of factious insubordination that took place in the 14th of the line had been very much exaggerated. Even before he received the War Minister's letter Colonel Bugeaud had written to the prefect of the Loire to deny them. The prefect had immediately forwarded Colonel Bugeaud's protest to the minister's office. The Minister-at-War received the document from the prefect on the same day that he had addressed to Colonel Bugeaud the missive given above. He immediately wrote a second letter to the Colonel, thus expressed, to be found, like the former, among the archives of the office of the Minister-at-War:

Paris, 17 March, 1815

Monsieur le Colonel,

I have this moment received, with a letter from the prefect of the Loire, a copy of that in which you complain of the disadvantageous reports current as to the bad spirit of some soldiers of your regiment. A report has indeed reached me on this matter, that led me to write directly to you on this very day. I am glad to learn that this report has no sort of foundation, and that you, your body of officers, and all the soldiers under your orders, are animated by feelings that give the greatest assurance of their fidelity to his Majesty. I will cause inquiry to be made for the authors of these false reports.

From these documents it clearly appears, therefore, that if Colonel Bugeaud joined in the rising of the Hundred Days, he did not in the least take the initiative. He gave his adhesion when the event had taken place; and setting aside the question of dynasty, there only remained the military and national question against the reconstituted coalition.

But, though quite false, these reports had the fatal effect of causing Colonel Bugeaud to be treated as an enemy and object of suspicion under the Restoration. Thus it was that the government of Louis XVIII. and the country were deprived of an able servant. M. de Lacombe adds:

I learn from a very trustworthy source that a very royalist officer, Commandant Count l'Esclaibes, who was a friend of Colonel Bugeaud, and knew his bravery and his sentiments, wished to put an end to this unjust disgrace, and give this valuable support to the monarchy. After the Hundred Days at the Tuileries he presented Colonel Bugeaud to the Duke d'Angoulême, president of the high commission on the army. The conversation was excellent and left a good impression, but unfortunately had no practical result.

In the correspondence of the Count de Chambord there is the following letter in which that prince expresses his rejoicing at the patriotic inclinations of Marshal Bugeaud; and adds that Colonel d'Esclaibes had long ago informed him of them:

Venice, 13 October, 1848.
To Monsieur X

I take advantage, my dear friend, of a safe opportunity to thank you for the various letters you have sent, me for some time. I have read with much interest the accounts you give me of the condition of things and minds; but what has struck me most is to see men of courage and ability of different parties forgetting their old divisions, and uniting in their efforts to save society from approaching destruction. This is a happy symptom that should confirm our hopes for the future. I am especially rejoiced at what you told me of the good disposition of Marshal Bugeaud. I am not surprised at it, for the excellent, Colonel d'Esclaibes, whom we have had the misfortune to lose and who was his friend, had taught me to know him long ago. By his military talents, his great ability, his firm and energetic character, and the influence he exercises over the army, the Marshal may be called to render the most signal services to our country, under existing circumstances. As for me, whose motto has always been "Everything for France," my wish, my sole ambition, you know, is to serve my country, to devote myself to her and those who will assist me to save her, and give her rest, freedom, prosperity, and greatness. Such men may always count upon my entire recognition. They will always find me ready to hold out a hand to them, wherever they may come from.
Henry

CHAPTER 10
The Hundred Days (1815)

The return of the Emperor from the Island of Elba had again kindled the war in Europe, and the frontiers of France were bristling afresh with a hedge of bayonets. The 14th of the line, which was intended to form the advanced guard of the army of the Alps, was still under the orders of Marshal Suchet, and had, this time, to contend with the Austro-Sardinian army holding the valleys and defiles of Savoy. Our military glory, so soon destined to be obscured upon the field of Waterloo, darted forth a last flash upon the frontiers of Italy, and it was to the brave colonel of the 14th of the line that we owe this heroic feat of arms.

This glorious incident of war, remaining almost unknown amid the frightful crash of the colossus of empire falling into ruins, seems to us like one of those final radiances that sometimes illumine the sky as the orb of day is vanishing. Might not there be a curious similitude in the idea that the young colonel who, in an obscure corner of Savoy, just before the disaster of Waterloo, accomplished the last gallant action that adorned the imperial era, should, after a long enforced sleep of fifteen years, awake as the most accomplished soldier of his time, the only great warrior of the monarchy of 1830?

The commencement of hostilities had been fixed for the 15th of June. The 14th, which was stationed at Chatelard, among the mountains of Banges, in Savoy, had received orders to descend into the valley of Tarentaise, guarded by a Piedmontese corps, and to take possession of the small towns of Conflans and l'Hôpital.

It was then that Colonel Bugeaud, in conformity with orders received, attempted one of those bold strokes in which he had so often succeeded in Spain. A battalion of the enemy (*batallion* Comte Robert), was established as advanced picket at Saint Pierre d'Albigny. Colonel Bugeaud resolved to surround it, and make it prisoner with hardly a blow. With this object he despatched three companies by a mountain-path that came out about half a league in rear of the village, and ordered them to lay in wait. Then he attacked in front with the rest of his force. One part of the enemy's detachment was captured or killed, the rest ran away and fell into the ambuscade prepared; not a man escaped, and by four in the morning the whole Piedmontese battalion was captured.

In this combat Colonel Bugeaud himself made two prisoners, who turned out to be two Frenchmen, MM. de Polignac and de Macarthy, commissioners of Louis XVIII., with the Austro-Sardinian army.

We will leave the account of it to Colonel Bugeaud, who relates this episode in a letter addressed to one of his sisters, dated August 3. A Piedmontese brigade, 3,000 men strong, had come in haste to support its advanced picket, getting no communication from it. It came in contact with the victorious 14th, was routed after a pretty sharp conflict, and retired, leaving with its opponent, 200 prisoners, its wounded, its dead, and the possession of the towns of Conflans and l'Hôpital, not even attempting to defend the approaches, which the 14th occupied conformably to orders received.

Some days later Colonel Bugeaud, seeing that the enemy continued to commit the same blunder, and that their advanced posts did not sufficiently guard their lines of communication with the main body of their troops, again gave himself the pleasure of capturing a battalion posted at Moutiers as an outlying picket. He employed the same method that had previously been successful, brought upon the enemy's line of retreat a detachment which had to march for eleven hours by horrible roads, then attacking the picket in front, took it between two fires, and forced it to surrender.

It would seem that Marshal Bugeaud must afterwards have especially had the remembrance of these two exploits in his mind, when he wrote in his *Maxims of the Art of War:*

Efficient guards must always be distant, and equally must it be impossible for the enemy to penetrate through the chain of the advanced posts unobserved. A fault often committed by the chief of a detachment posted on outlying picket, at a great distance from a numerous force, is to surround himself with precautions calculated to prevent himself from being surprised, but to leave behind him a considerable space in which a party of the enemy may lie in wait, and fall upon the detachment when it, attacked by superior force from another side, thinks it can easily retire to its own forces, then it is captured, and uncovers the space it was ordered to occupy.

This was a happy commencement for the army of the Alps; to be followed by a combat still more glorious, that might have gained a great reputation, had not at the very moment the bloody day of Waterloo absorbed the attention of France and the whole of Europe by the vastness of the strife of which it was the turning-point, and the incalculable consequences that followed it. But it does not displease us, while turning over this grand page of history, to tarry, in company with the valiant man of war whose life we are endeavouring to describe, among these combats obscure, but deserving illustration, that so honourably terminated the war upon our Alpine frontiers. Besides, there can be no doubt that the remembrance of this success was especially valued by the Marshal when he reached an advanced age, full of honours, for he gave a very full account of it in an anonymous pamphlet printed, in 1845, at the Government press at Algiers, from which we take some of the details that follow.

In the last days of the month of June, 1815, the 14th of the line, reinforced by a battalion of the 20th of the line, still held the two towns of Conflans and l'Hôpital, washed by the stream of the Arly, a small tributary of the Isere. Some prisoners, made on the 26th, informed Colonel Bugeaud that he was to be a attacked two days afterwards by 10,000 Austrians under the orders of General Trenck, coming down the Little Saint Bernard, while General Bubna, coming from Mont Cenis with 20,000 men, was to advance by the valley of Maurienne, held on one side by the brigade of General Mesclop.

Colonel Bugeaud lost no time in forwarding this information to the General-in-chief, and judiciously requested that Mesclop's brigade might come and join him without delay in the valley of the Tarentaise, so as to combine their efforts to crush General Trenck, while Bubna's column 'should strike at nothing, and run its head against the *tête-de-pont* of Montmeillan.' But Marshal Suchet had already received intelligence of the disaster at Waterloo, and, considering it useless to prolong hostilities, had sent a proposal for an armistice to General Bubna. Being convinced that this proposal would be accepted, and the forward march of the Austrian corps stopped, he gave no orders to the 14th of the line or to Mesclop's brigade.

On the morning of the 28th, instead of the reinforcement so ardently desired, Colonel Bugeaud received the official bulletin of the battle of Waterloo, and, by a singular coincidence, the deputation of the regiment which had been sent to the Champ de Mars for the distribution of the eagles, joined at the same moment, bringing the eagle for the regiment, together with the account of the Emperor's abdication.

While these unfavourable reports were spreading through the ranks, and causing great excitement, a sub-officer of cavalry arrived at full speed and brought information of the approach of the Austrians. Matters looked grave; resistance to an enemy of considerable numerical superiority, with soldiers disconcerted and troubled by the cruel intelligence just received, might have seemed a hazardous enterprise; but Colonel Bugeaud, inspired by ardent patriotism alone, found some noble words that went to the soldiers' hearts, and restored their morale.

Forming up his regiment in close column, he himself read the bulletin of Waterloo, and received the eagle in the name of the country, speaking these words in a loud voice:

'Soldiers of the 14th line, here is your eagle. It is in the name of the country that I present it to you, for if the Emperor, as here stated, is no longer our sovereign, France remains. She it is who confides this standard to you; it will always be your talisman of victory. Swear that as long as a soldier of the 14th exists no enemy's hand shall touch it!'

'We swear it,' cried all the soldiers, and the officers stepped from the ranks, waving their swords and shouting again, 'We swear it!'

It was in this mood that the 14th was going to meet the enemy.

In order the better to resist such superior forces, Colonel Bugeaud proposed only to defend the right flank of the Arly, and to allow the enemy to pass the stream in small bodies, so as to have them on easier terms, and crush them in detail. He began by a slack defence of the positions on the left bank, so as to prevent the enemy from adopting a plan that they might have conceived if they had met with an energetic resistance, that of crossing the Arly at some distance and turning the position. With the same view he prevented the destruction of the bridge that unites Conflans and l'Hôpital. The event was as he had foreseen. When the Austrians had made themselves masters of the left bank, which had been so easily abandoned to them, they several times endeavoured to debouch from the bridge.

Every time they were received by a sharp fire from a short distance; then our troops quitting their shelter advanced upon the enemy with the bayonet, and thrust them back to the other side of the stream with considerable loss.

Despairing of forcing the passage in this manner, the Austrians passed a column of two thousand men over a ford below the town, intending to cut the line of retreat of the defenders of l'Hôpital. Colonel Bugeaud, not choosing to empty the little town, only made use of six companies of the centre to meet this movement. Though numerically inferior, the want of numbers was compensated for by an excess of audacity, and he flung these few men, with himself, upon the rear of the enemy's column, so that they, thinking that they themselves were threatened with being cut off from the ford where they had crossed the river, became demoralised, gave back, and were flung in disorder into the Isere and the Arly, having sustained a considerable loss by a well-sustained and well-directed fire. A second attempt of the same kind on another point was not more successful.

However, cartridges began to fail, and the Colonel would perhaps have decided upon retiring, if he had not been reluctant to leave to the enemy's mercy a battalion of the 67th that had on the sound of the engagement made its way by the valley of Udine and had just communicated with him.

Not being able to maintain himself any longer in l'Hôpital without ammunition, Colonel Bugeaud rallied his men, and made them take up positions on the hills in the rear. The Austrians entered the deserted town and pillaged it. Meanwhile a detachment of twenty mules loaded with cartridges had been brought up; the pouches were filled, and the battalion of the 67th came up with some pieces of artillery. Their arrival was a signal to take

121

the offensive; the 14th again rushed forward, killed or captured 1,500 Austrians who occupied l'Hôpital, and effected its junction with the battalion of the 67th over a heap of corpses.

At the same moment a battalion of the 20th of the line arrived by the Chambery road. Colonel Bugeaud, seeing his force augmented by two battalions, prepared to cross the Arly in his turn, and to complete the destruction of the Austrian division, when an officer from the headquarters' staff arrived with the information that the armistice was signed, and, to his great regret, the intrepid Bugeaud had to break off the movement just begun. But he gave himself the pleasure of waiting till the enemy themselves sent him information of the armistice, and thus had the well-deserved satisfaction of not leaving the field of battle till the next day.

So terminated this combat in which 1,750 French fought for ten hours against nearly 10,000 Austrians, killed 2,000 men of them, and made 960 prisoners.

After the disaster of Waterloo, 18th June, 1815, and the second abdication of the Emperor Napoleon I., 23rd June, 1815, according to the conventions with the allied armies, the French forces were to retire behind the Loire, and Marshal Suchet's corps to quit Savoy.

A letter from Colonel Bugeaud, written to his sister, on 3rd August, 1815, is already a foreboding of the adverse decision about to be made with regard to him.

TO HIS SISTER PHILLIS

Saint-Symphorien, 3rd August, 1815: I received your letter of 20th July at Saint-Symphorien. The one you addressed to me at the army of the Loire has not reached me yet. Your opinion agrees with mine. When I recovered from the first moment of disgust, I considered that it was right to wait at my post till I am told, 'Be off with you!', and that then I should have a right to say, 'I served my country as long as

I could, and it is not my fault that I am not serving it still.'
I fully expect that we shall be discharged, the proscriptions
do not promise anything good.

I should not be sorry to remain upon half-pay for a year
or two while things settle themselves.

Our army is obedient indeed; very obedient. Some days
since we received the white cockade. I have resumed this
badge in the regiment without encountering fresh desertions.

You may feel sure I never will join in a civil war unless
compelled by persecution. I am too much of a Frenchman
ever to shed the blood of my fellow citizens as long as they
do not threaten my life.

I am in daily expectation of leaving this country and
going to Clermont. You can write to me at Roanne till
further directions; your letter will follow me.

You will no doubt like to see our deed of submission; I
send you an exact copy of it:

> *Sire,*
>
> *The officers, sub-officers, and private soldiers of the 14th
> Regiment of the line, present to Your Majesty the homage of
> their complete submission. We unreservedly range ourselves
> under the banner of the lilies. The fate of the country is
> henceforth combined with that of your sacred person. This
> fact will be the warranty of our fidelity and love.*
>
> *May all Frenchmen, forgetting their divisions, only make
> one great family, and have like us but one cry, "Long live the
> King, and France in all its integrity!"*
>
> *You will experience our devotion, Sire, if ever this integ-
> rity should be threatened.*

I have received a long and kind letter from Hélène, and
answered it. Ask her for my letter of the end of July, it will
interest you. I give her accounts that I have not sent you;
in your turn I am going to give you some that she has not
received, and you may send her in exchange.

On the 15th of June, at two in the morning, I surprised the Piedmontese advanced posts at Saint-Pierre d'Albigny. I entered the town with the first of the Voltigeurs. I heard two men galloping away down the street. Having no mounted men I pursued them myself, and cutting them off at the turn of the road, I made them prisoners.

'Who are you?'

'French travellers.'

'French travellers at such an hour, armed and in the enemy's lines. I cannot recognise you as such. No, gentlemen, you are not Frenchmen.'

'Yes, sir, we are; and as we must tell you, we are French émigrés. We left our country to escape from Bonaparte and serve the King.'

'Ah, I understand, you are royalists, but foreigners and not citizens of France.'

'Sir, we are Frenchmen on honour; we are on the road to it, and it is not very clear that you are on the same course.'

'Gentlemen, do not compel me to abuse the power I have over you and say harsh things, which your own conduct may easily give occasion to. We will break this off: You will be taken to headquarters with the other prisoners, and you will be able to explain to Marshal Suchet.'

I was in haste, and went on my way without ascertaining the names of my prisoners. In the evening I heard that one of them was M. Jules de Polignac, and the other M. de Macarthy of Toulouse; that they had been several days upon the frontier establishing communications with France, and giving information to the Piedmontese of all the movements of the French army.

The Marshal had them taken to Fort Bareau; but I soon learnt that they had quietly been set at liberty.

Three or four days ago I received a letter from M. Macarthy asking me to let him have for 1,000 francs a couple of carriage-horses belonging to him, which I had taken in the affair of Saint-Pierre.

I answered him, that considering the Macarthys of Toulouse are relations to those of Bordeaux, who are my cousins, I could not consider these horses as fair booty, and that he might send for them, not for the 1,000 francs, but for nothing.

I added something, to say that this was not the least in consequence of circumstances, but owing to the name of Macarthy.

To his sister Phillis

Clermont, 27th August, 1815: Progress is being made with our disbandment. This will take up at least a month, and will delay by so long the pleasure I shall have in pressing you in my arms.

The councils of administration will be provisionally kept up, to give in their accounts with the records and stores. That of the 14th is to be merged in the legion of the department of Côte-d'Or, and said to be intended for the nucleus. If any colonels receive employment in each legion, I am almost assured I shall be among those chosen. The Marshal has told me several times, 'If anyone in the army ought to be employed, it is you.'

As soon as we are disbanded, if circumstances permit, I will go and see you. I shall travel on horseback by cross-roads.

You will be glad to hear that several persons of distinction of the department of the Loire have joined in requesting their deputies to ask the King to give me the legion of the Loire. I have letters to this effect from M. de Montenac, and the Marquis de Talame, peer of France. I do not reckon much on its success, but am flattered at this proof of good-will which I owe to the good conduct of my regiment, and to a slight service that I did to the people of the country. This is it. A band of Austrian hussars were wasting the country, pillaging, robbing, violating, &c. I went after them with eight mounted officers. We caught them at the village of Regny, and took them all.

I have received a long and kind letter from Hélène. She thinks a great deal about me.

The people of the South, or at least the royalists, are covering themselves with shame by a quantity of murders. They seem to wish to defy the Duke d'Angoulême rather than the King. They are in a complete state of anarchy.

The illegitimate sovereign's party did not commit such crimes. I hope that as soon as His Majesty can he will chastise these brigands with white and green cockades. Doubtless you know all that goes on in these countries. At Toulouse they murdered the General the King had sent.

In several other places the authorities appointed by the King have been unable to enter upon their duties.

Love to your husband, to Julien, to all the family, and to all the friends.

You do not tell me about my money. Will Granger pay me?

On the 16th of September, 1815, as he had foreseen, Colonel Bugeaud was disbanded, as a brigand of the Loire, and ceased to belong to the army. Perhaps we may find an explanation of this proceeding on comparing it with an incident that is rather obscure, for unfortunately no letter of the Marshal's nor any formal document gives information about it.

We have seen that the former major of the Spanish wars had received his colonel's rank from Louis XVIII., 11th of June, 1814. There is no reason to doubt the sincerity of the Royalist feelings displayed by him at Orleans. The son of the Marquis de la Piconnerie had, besides, no strong bonds of gratitude to attach him to the Emperor. Then came the Hundred Days. Together with the whole army the Colonel took his place beneath the standards of the usurper, and, under the orders of his commanding officer, proceeded to join him with his regiment at Auxerre.

What took place afterwards? The Colonel of the 14th of the line must have had some powerful enemies in the office of the Minister-at-War, for they managed to deprive him of his regiment. The order was given by the minister, but not carried into effect. Why? The curious autograph letter of the Emperor now in our hands will tell us.

Monsieur le Colonel Bugeaud,

I am satisfied with your conduct. The command of the 14th Regiment of the line, with which you joined me at Auxerre has wrongfully been taken from you. I have given orders for it to be restored to you, and in proof of my satisfaction have appointed you Commander of the Legion of Honour.

Napoleon

Paris, 8th May, 1815

Let us endeavour to establish the facts. No doubt this must have passed, perhaps even without the knowledge of Colonel Bugeaud. His protector, Marshal Suchet, who showed an especial appreciation of the brilliant soldier of the Catalonian army, had been informed of the injustice about to be inflicted upon his comrade in arms, and managed to obviate it. He was easily able to persuade the Emperor to revoke his minister's decision, by showing him how important it was at that critical moment to favour and secure to his side such a valiant soldier as Colonel Bugeaud. Thence arose the imperial letter and the quite unexpected nomination as commander of the Legion of Honour.

Indeed, Thomas Bugeaud, Chevalier of the Legion of Honour in 1811, had been made an officer of the order on March 17, 1815. Two months afterwards he was Commander! This politic nomination was a dexterous action of

Napoleon I, who evidently wished by an especial favour to attach to himself one of the youngest, cleverest, and most steady colonels in the army.

We have seen at Conflans and l'Hôpital in what brilliant fashion Bugeaud showed that he deserved the high distinction which imperial favour, by a kind of divination and prescience, had granted him beforehand. Notwithstanding the Colonel's fine feat of arms, notwithstanding his services, his name and his friends, it is certain that after Waterloo and Napoleon I's abdication, his determined enemies at the War Office produced, at the right moment, this unexceptionable proof of the good-will of the usurper, and took advantage of it to procure the insertion of Colonel Bugeaud's name among those who were discharged.

CHAPTER 11

Country Life

This period of fifteen years, 1815 to 1830, during which the brilliant soldier found himself compelled, by events, to abandon military life, was far from being idle. The brave, indefatigable officer carried with him into his retirement the same ardour, devotion, and activity, that had already filled the first part of his life. Besides, this was not the first time he had engaged in agriculture, and farming had long ago attracted him. We have told how it was that several years before he had missed breaking off his career, and devoting himself entirely to the management of his little domain.

In 1815, the object of his life was to be completely changed. We find in his manuscript notes, a sort of biography dictated by himself to one of his daughters, the account of his first attempts, and the inauguration of the first agricultural society established in France.

Struck with the wretchedness of the people of my country, I found the cause in the system of agriculture, namely, fallowing in its most primitive state. I saw that if I could not serve the State with my sword, I might still be useful to the country-people by teaching them how to improve their condition by a more intelligent system of labour. I undertook this mission with infinite eagerness, and it had a great effect in consoling me for the loss of a career that offered me the most brilliant prospects.

A lady, as good as she was beautiful, soon united her lot to mine, and the soldier was nothing more than a most active and zealous agriculturist. By daybreak I was in the fields leading my labourers, and showing them how the work ought to be done.

In order to speak with more authority, I had very speedily learnt how to hold the plough, use the scythe, and all the agricultural implements as dexterously as the most practised workman. And I especially opened the minds of the tillers of the soil by my teaching, and stirred up the neighbouring townsfolk to a taste for agriculture.

However, I soon perceived that if my efforts stood alone, they would not be able to conquer the bad habits that had been the rule for centuries. My idea, therefore, was to unite all the landowners of the canton into a society. As soon as I could show a favourable specimen of the effects of the course of cropping that I had selected with reference to the nature of the soil and climate, I assembled all my neighbours. After a breakfast, there was an inspection of the fields; they were delighted with the excellence of my artificial grasses, roots, and all my cultivation of a kind quite new to the country. Actually, enthusiasm was displayed, for no one believed that these lands were capable of producing such things.

I had previously prepared papers for the formation of a company, and a programme of the encouragement to be given to agriculture in the canton, and I took advantage of the general feeling to lay it before the party, and all present signed. Thus was organized the first agricultural society of La Dordogne, and I believe in France: this took place in 1819.

The society prospered, and caused such progress to be made in the canton as astonished the neighbouring cantons. I stirred them up to imitation, and had the happiness of becoming the promoter and organizer of several other societies.

At the beginning of the year 1818, Colonel Bugeaud married Mdlle. de Lafaye, of one of the most respected families in the country. Here is a very interesting letter addressed by the impatient betrothed to his future father-in-law, in which the Colonel describes his whole self with original and delightful frankness.

<u>To his Father-in-Law</u>

Excideuil, 27 October, 1817: I trust you will excuse a very natural impatience in one who aspires to the happiness of becoming a member of your family. It is impossible for me to wait till St. Martin's day to ask from you an answer upon which my happiness depends. You had the kindness to promise it to me in a few days. It is only indirectly that I have learnt that you have fixed a more distant period. You had not told me; I may then surely beg you to fulfil your first promise, without your being able to impute indiscretion to me. And why should you defer a moment so much desired by me?

Shall you know me better in a fortnight? Have you not had time enough for consideration? Have you not been able to get all possible information? In mercy, sir, do not, defer giving me a certainty. Consult your own heart; it will tell you, for it is kind, that you cannot leave me longer in this cruel expectation.

But it is especially your daughter whom you must consult, if you have not already done so. I hold above everything to her own well considered choice; otherwise there will be no happiness. I am also sure that you will do nothing distasteful to her; your intentions on this matter are well enough known, and your character would point them out.

I know that some persons have cast doubts upon my temper. Soldiers are said to be generally despots, being used to command; I can only refute this idea by defending myself and my comrades. I will therefore confine myself to observing that there is no military man who is not under command more, perhaps, than he is in command, and that this graduated subordination beginning with the private and only terminating with the chief of the state, teaches all to obey as well as to command. Assuredly a rich only son, who has never left home, has much more the habit of absolute command than a Marshal of France, and it would be a good thing for spoilt children to be in the service for four or five years. I fancy their tempers would be improved by it.

My fortune is not what M. Festugiéres thought, upon what grounds I know not, for I have never exaggerated it beyond the reality. I have 78,000 francs either in my pocket-book or well invested. I will immediately make a, purchase to that amount, if you require it. I have, besides, my pay, worth about 8,000 francs. I allow that this is little in the general way of considering these things. Your daughter is more wealthy: I wish she were not so well off, or that I were more so, and that would be better. However, my means are sufficient according to all my wants; and I should not desire any more unless it might be as a means of levelling the difficulties that stand in the way of a union that I desire more than I have ever wished for anything in the world.

My messenger has orders to wait for your answer till tomorrow; I reckon upon your kindness not to keep me in suspense any longer.

Colonel Bugeaud having returned home, where he soon became head of his family, could not remain inactive. His vivid imagination, elevated mind, and heart always full of a wish to do good, required occupation to make him forget the field of battle. He soon found it. An immense sphere was opening before him. Limousin where he was born, Périgord the land of his adoption, were then far from being reckoned among our most fertile provinces. There was widespread misery. As we are told by M. de Bezancenetz, an Algerian, an actual worshipper of Marshal Bugeaud:

The colonel looked around, he saw a land sparsely covered with heather, further off vast lands without vegetation, scorched up as if wasted by fire, with only a crop of grey rocks like the bones of an abandoned cemetery. He Looked another way; on the hill, meagre vine stock s only just pushed forth their stunted branches; in the valley, marshy meadows scarcely produced sedges enough to feed the few lean cows dolefully browsing there. Here a scanty chestnut-grove with mutilated trees; there a copse-wood with foliage turning yellow before its time. The veteran of thirty was greatly excited. He went to see if the arable land was in better condition: alas, half of it was fallow, and what had been turned by the plough seemed only to promise half profits to the cultivators.

The Colonel reached a farmhouse by a broken-up road, choked with rolling stones, furrowed with ruts. Children in rags, half naked, played upon the manure-heap where the fowls scratched and the pigs routed. He entered the house by a broken door. The only openings of the one habitable room were two small windows, without casements, and only provided with an inside shutter closed at night when there was no need for light. Thick planks put together into the shape of chests, covered with straw and a few rags over them, were made to serve as two beds for the use of the whole family; an old worm-eaten chest, a bread-board, two benches and two stools, completed the farmer's furniture. The floor was of uneven, trodden earth, the stairs were a step-ladder leading to an almost empty loft. Such was the appearance of the farmhouses of Périgord in 1815, when the disbanded colonel came to take up his residence in the country.

He who now travels in the country colonised by M. Bugeaud, cannot imagine that in so short a space of time as fifteen years the aspect of the country could have been so changed by the influence of one single man. When he admires the fields with such even furrows, and covered with flourishing crops of corn, the artificial meadows with such rich, thick sward, the main roads thickly metalled, the smiling and comfortable farms, the healthy and well-clothed villagers, he cannot believe that this plenty and prosperity only dates from some twenty years back. Why should it not be so? The very inhabitants of the country being used to the miracle, only have a confused remembrance of the past.

Colonel Bugeaud's attempts had at first been viewed with mistrust. When the peasants saw him undoing and destroying everything in his domains, they shook their heads, and the owners of property boldly declared that the innovator would ruin himself. Each new trial, every implement unknown in the country, were the objects of malignant curiosity and criticism from all. What was the use of those harrows? Their teeth would never break the clods as well as the old peasant's mattock. What was the use of these stone-rollers, to part the grain from the Straw? The flail known from all ages did its work much better. Did not the Colonel also entertain the crazy notion of having the harvested corn trodden under the feet of horses on the threshing-floor? Clearly the Colonel was possessed with a mania for novelties that would bring him to ruin and the most melancholy results.

But when, after a few years, the most obstinate could no longer keep out the light, when they saw that instead of being ruined, the innovator had considerably increased his income, there was a truce to disparagement. People even began to allow that M. Bugeaud sometimes had good notions, and at last came imitation. This was what the Colonel waited for. The improvement of his own property was only half his projected work; his wish was to regenerate the *canton*, the *arrondissement*, the whole department.

He had rebuilt his houses; the men who worked for him were better clothed, better fed, more intelligent than their like. Again, by his care a school for the children of his commune had been established in a house of his own. But that was not enough; the good must be propagated from neighbour to neighbour, like contagious diseases of other days. So the Colonel, far from repulsing those who seemed inclined to proceed with him on the course he was pursuing with so much success, placed himself entirely at their disposal. He helped them with his advice, gradually brought them to his views, and one morning, as he has told us himself, the agricultural society was founded.

It was a great day for Colonel Bugeaud. In his ideas the existence of an agricultural society was a fountain of prosperity to the country to whose progress and welfare it was devoted. He said, 'Agriculture being a science of local practice, the clever men of the locality must select the processes most suitable to the different localities. This is the original idea of agricultural societies.'

It was not in his own department alone that he desired to establish these gatherings of practical agriculturists, but all over France; later, he moved in the Chamber that a sum of two million francs should be allotted for promoting the establishment of similar institutions in all the *cantons* of France, so that two hundred thousand persons might be morally associated in the same work of regeneration. His dream was realised; and under the Second Empire annual district agricultural society meetings were established throughput our territory. Never should it be forgotten that this idea, so simple and so fruitful in results, is due to the initiative of Colonel Bugeaud.

He said on one occasion in the Chamber:

It is all very well to colonise Algeria, but it would be still more interesting to colonise the great plains of Brittany and Bordeaux. A portion of the army might be thus employed, and villages built there, on the camp principle, but on a convenient plan for agricultural work; the troops might occupy them with the double object of being taught the art of war, and of cultivating the adjacent land. When the ground had been brought into such a state that families could live upon it, these villages and their dependencies might be sold or leased out.

Some persons who have not observed the vast resources of agriculture are uneasy at the increase of population. It is said there are too many people; I will undertake to prove there are not enough. We could feed, and feed better, more than twice as many. Certainly the population is at this moment ill arranged. There are too many in the towns, but I would undertake to employ all the excess of Lyons, Bordeaux, Rouen, Marseilles, and Paris, in the country of Limoges.

These notions of the 'soldier labourer' spread in the neighbourhood. The seed bore fruit, and his example and advice were so well followed, that the *canton* of Lanouaille soon became, from an agricultural point of view, one of the most advanced parts of half the central provinces, and of the entire south. The movement did not stop there, and the mode of cultivation that he advocated spread over Périgord and some of the Limousin; agricultural societies were established in several *cantons*, and the whole country presented a new aspect.

Colonel Bugeaud was adored by the peasants. His address being affable, encouraging, and grave, and his fatherly solicitude had a great share in the success of his enterprise for agricultural and moral regeneration. He succeeded in improving their generous but rather hasty natures. So the peasant of Périgord still carefully retains in his memory the recollection of the master of La Durantie. In his familiar talk by the farm fireside, on a bundle; of straw in the barn, before the church, as on the occasion of the rural solemnities at the distribution of premiums, his language was simple, energetic, and plain. He always contrived to teach the labourers a great deal they did not know, and to correct their ideas about what they knew imperfectly. He talked familiarly with them, politics, work, agriculture, even social economy, so as to make them understand the hardest questions.

Amid these absorbing occupations and pure enjoyments did the years of the Restoration pass with Colonel Bugeaud. He took but little part in politics, refusing to be present at such republican and Bonapartist meetings as kept alight the holy fire of the revolution at Perigeux and Limoges.

The young Colonel, though he had been so stupidly set aside by the Government of the Restoration, did not feel any aversion to it. In fact, he could reckon among the influential men of the day some intimate and devoted friends, who bitterly deplored that so many brilliant and solid qualities should be buried deep in Périgord, and never guessed the wonders and transformations accomplished in his province by this able man, with his energy and perseverance.

[So it was that Bugeaud returned to his first love, agriculture. The sword had not yet, however, been turned to the ploughshare and another call to his country's colours and more battles lay ahead. The soldier had not yet become the farmer! *The Leonaur Editors.*]

LEONAUR

ALSO FROM LEONAUR

AVAILABLE IN SOFTCOVER OR HARDCOVER WITH DUST JACKET

CAPTAIN OF THE 95th (Rifles) *by Jonathan Leach*—An officer of Wellington's Sharpshooters during the Peninsular, South of France and Waterloo Campaigns of the Napoleonic Wars.

THE KHAKEE RESSALAH *by Robert Henry Wallace Dunlop*—Service & adventure with the Meerut volunteer horse during the Indian mutiny 1857-1858

BUGLER AND OFFICER OF THE RIFLES *by William Green & Harry Smith* With the 95th (Rifles) during the Peninsular & Waterloo Campaigns of the Napoleonic Wars

BAYONETS, BUGLES AND BONNETS *by James 'Thomas' Todd*—Experiences of hard soldiering with the 71st Foot - the Highland Light Infantry - through many battles of the Napoleonic wars including the Peninsular & Waterloo Campaigns

A NORFOLK SOLDIER IN THE FIRST SIKH WAR *by J W Baldwin*—Experiences of a private of H.M. 9th Regiment of Foot in the battles for the Punjab, India 1845-46

A CAVALRY OFFICER DURING THE SEPOY REVOLT *by A.R.D. Mackenzie*—Experiences with the 3rd Bengal Light Cavalry, the Guides and Sikh Irregular Cavalry from the outbreak to Delhi and Lucknow

THE ADVENTURES OF A LIGHT DRAGOON *by George Farmer & G.R. Gleig*—A cavalryman during the Peninsular & Waterloo Campaigns, in captivity & at the siege of Bhurtpore, India

THE COMPLEAT RIFLEMAN HARRIS *by Benjamin Harris as told to & transcribed by Captain Henry Curling*—The adventures of a soldier of the 95th (Rifles) during the Peninsular Campaign of the Napoleonic Wars

THE RED DRAGOON *by W.J. Adams*—With the 7th Dragoon Guards in the Cape of Good Hope against the Boers & the Kaffir tribes during the 'war of the axe' 1843-48

THE LIFE OF THE REAL BRIGADIER GERARD - Volume 1 - THE YOUNG HUSSAR 1782 - 1807 *by Jean-Baptiste De Marbot*—A French Cavalryman Of the Napoleonic Wars at Marengo, Austerlitz, Jena, Eylau & Friedland

THE LIFE OF THE REAL BRIGADIER GERARD Volume 2 IMPERIAL AIDE-DE-CAMP 1807 - 1811 *by Jean-Baptiste De Marbot*—A French Cavalryman of the Napoleonic Wars at Saragossa, Landshut, Eckmuhl, Ratisbon, Aspern-Essling, Wagram, Busaco & Torres Vedras

AVAILABLE ONLINE AT
www.leonaur.com
AND OTHER GOOD BOOK STORES

LEONAUR

ALSO FROM LEONAUR

AVAILABLE IN SOFTCOVER OR HARDCOVER WITH DUST JACKET

SEPOYS, SIEGE & STORM *by Charles John Griffiths*—The Experiences of a young officer of H.M.'s 61st Regiment at Ferozepore, Delhi ridge and at the fall of Delhi during the Indian mutiny 1857.

CAMPAIGNING IN ZULULAND *by W. E. Montague*—Experiences on campaign during the Zulu war of 1879 with the 94th Regiment.

THE STORY OF THE GUIDES *by G. J. Younghusband*—The Exploits of the Soldiers of the famous Indian Army Regiment from the northwest frontier 1847 - 1900..

ZULU: 1879 *by D.C.F. Moodie & the Leonaur Editors*—The Anglo-Zulu War of 1879 from contemporary sources: First Hand Accounts, Interviews, Dispatches, Official Documents & Newspaper Reports.

THE RECOLLECTIONS OF SKINNER OF SKINNER'S HORSE *by James Skinner*—James Skinner and his 'Yellow Boys' Irregular cavalry in the wars of India between the British, Mahratta, Rajput, Mogul, Sikh & Pindarree Forces.

TOMMY ATKINS' WAR STORIES 14 FIRST HAND ACCOUNTS—Fourteen first hand accounts from the ranks of the British Army during Queen Victoria's Empire Original & True Battle Stories Recollections of the Indian Mutiny With the 49th in the Crimea With the Guards in Egypt The Charge of the Six Hundred With Wolseley in Ashanti Alma, Inkermann and Magdala With the Gunners at Tel-el-Kebir Russian Guns and Indian Rebels Rough Work in the Crimea In the Maori Rising Facing the Zulus From Sebastopol to Lucknow Sent to Save Gordon On the March to Chitral Tommy by Rudyard Kipling

CHASSEUR OF 1914 *by Marcel Dupont*—Experiences of the twilight of the French Light Cavalry by a young officer during the early battles of the great war in Europe.

TROOP HORSE & TRENCH *by R. A. Lloyd*—The experiences of a British Lifeguardsman of the household cavalry fighting on the western front during the First World War 1914-18.

THE EAST AFRICAN MOUNTED RIFLES *by C. J. Wilson*—Experiences of the campaign in the East African bush during the First World War.

THE FIGHTING CAMELIERS *by Frank Reid*—The exploits of the Imperial Camel Corps in the desert and Palestine campaigns of the First World War.

LEONAUR

ALSO FROM LEONAUR
AVAILABLE IN SOFTCOVER OR HARDCOVER WITH DUST JACKET

THE COMPLEAT RIFLEMAN HARRIS *by Benjamin Harris as told to & transcribed by Captain Henry Curling*—The adventures of a soldier of the 95th (Rifles) during the Peninsular Campaign of the Napoleonic Wars

WITH WELLINGTON'S LIGHT CAVALRY *by William Tomkinson*—The Experiences of an officer of the 16th Light Dragoons in the Peninsular and Waterloo campaigns of the Napoleonic Wars.

SERGEANT BOURGOGNE *by Adrien Bourgogne*—With Napoleon's Imperial Guard in the Russian Campaign and on the Retreat from Moscow 1812 - 13.

SWORDS OF HONOUR *by Henry Newbolt & Stanley L. Wood*—The Careers of Six Outstanding Officers from the Napoleonic Wars, the Wars for India and the American Civil War, with dozens of illustrations by Stanley L. Wood.

SURTEES OF THE RIFLES *by William Surtees*—A Soldier of the 95th (Rifles) in the Peninsular campaign of the Napoleonic Wars.

ENSIGN BELL IN THE PENINSULAR WAR *by George Bell*—The Experiences of a young British Soldier of the 34th Regiment 'The Cumberland Gentlemen' in the Napoleonic wars.

HUSSAR IN WINTER *by Alexander Gordon*—A British Cavalry Officer during the retreat to Corunna in the Peninsular campaign of the Napoleonic Wars.

NAPOLEONIC WAR STORIES *by Sir Arthur Quiller-Couch*—Tales of soldiers, spies, battles & sieges from the Peninsular & Waterloo campaingns.

JOURNALS OF ROBERT ROGERS OF THE RANGERS *by Robert Rogers*—The exploits of Rogers & the Rangers in his own words during 1755-1761 in the French & Indian War.

KERSHAW'S BRIGADE VOLUME 1 *by D. Augustus Dickert*—Manassas, Seven Pines, Sharpsburg (Antietam), Fredricksburg, Chancellorsville, Gettysburg, Chickamauga, Chattanooga, Fort Sanders & Bean Station..

KERSHAW'S BRIGADE VOLUME 2 *by D. Augustus Dickert*—At the wilderness, Cold Harbour, Petersburg, The Shenandoah Valley and Cedar Creek.

A TIGER ON HORSEBACK *by L. March Phillips*—The Experiences of a Trooper & Officer of Rimington's Guides - The Tigers - during the Anglo-Boer war 1899 - 1902.

LEONAUR

ALSO FROM LEONAUR
AVAILABLE IN SOFTCOVER OR HARDCOVER WITH DUST JACKET

RGW1 RECOLLECTIONS OF THE GREAT WAR 1914 - 18
STEEL CHARIOTS IN THE DESERT by S. C. Rolls

The first world war experiences of a Rolls Royce armoured car driver with the Duke of Westminster in Libya and in Arabia with T.E. Lawrence.

SOFTCOVER : **ISBN 1-84677-005-X**
HARDCOVER : **ISBN 1-84677-019-X**

RGW2 RECOLLECTIONS OF THE GREAT WAR 1914 - 18
WITH THE IMPERIAL CAMEL CORPS IN THE GREAT WAR by Geoffrey Inchbald

The story of a serving officer with the British 2nd battalion against the Senussi and during the Palestine campaign.

SOFTCOVER : **ISBN 1-84677-007-6**
HARDCOVER : **ISBN 1-84677-012-2**

EW3 EYEWITNESS TO WAR SERIES
THE KHAKEE RESSALAH
by Robert Henry Wallace Dunlop

Service & adventure with the Meerut Volunteer Horse During the Indian Mutiny 1857-1858.

SOFTCOVER : **ISBN 1-84677-009-2**
HARDCOVER : **ISBN 1-84677-017-3**

WF1 THE WARFARE FICTION SERIES
NAPOLEONIC WAR STORIES
by Sir Arthur Quiller-Couch

Tales of soldiers, spies, battles & Sieges from the Peninsular & Waterloo campaigns

SOFTCOVER : **ISBN 1-84677-003-3**
HARDCOVER : **ISBN 1-84677-014-9**

ALSO FROM LEONAUR
AVAILABLE IN SOFTCOVER OR HARDCOVER WITH DUST JACKET

EW2 EYEWITNESS TO WAR SERIES
CAPTAIN OF THE 95th (Rifles) *by Jonathan Leach*

An officer of Wellington's Sharpshooters during the
Peninsular, South of France and Waterloo Campaigns
of the Napoleonic Wars.

SOFTCOVER : **ISBN 1-84677-001-7**
HARDCOVER : **ISBN 1-84677-016-5**

WFI THE WARFARE FICTION SERIES
NAPOLEONIC WAR STORIES
by Sir Arthur Quiller-Couch

Tales of soldiers, spies, battles & Sieges from the
Peninsular & Waterloo campaigns

SOFTCOVER : **ISBN 1-84677-003-3**
HARDCOVER : **ISBN 1-84677-014-9**

EWI EYEWITNESS TO WAR SERIES
RIFLEMAN COSTELLO *by Edward Costello*

The adventures of a soldier of the 95th (Rifles) in the
Peninsular & Waterloo Campaigns of the Napoleonic wars.

SOFTCOVER : **ISBN 1-84677-000-9**
HARDCOVER : **ISBN 1-84677-018-1**

MCI THE MILITARY COMMANDERS SERIES
**JOURNALS OF ROBERT ROGERS OF THE
RANGERS** *by Robert Rogers*

The exploits of Rogers & the Rangers in his own words
during 1755-1761 in the French & Indian War.

SOFTCOVER : **ISBN 1-84677-002-5**
HARDCOVER : **ISBN 1-84677-010-6**

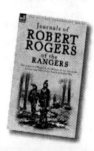

CPSIA information can be obtained at www.ICGtesting.com
Printed in the USA
LVOW060902280911

248236LV00001B/260/A